Advance praise for *Frientimacy*

"Every woman can relate to the feeling of having plenty of Facebook 'friends' or contacts to scroll through in her phone but still longing for the intimate connections she had with childhood friends, back when her BFF was her everything. I know I can. As I read through Nelson's description of why women experience loneliness—because we lack close connections, not because we don't know enough people—I found myself wondering how she got in my head. Anyone who has admired intimate friendships in pop culture and wondered *Why don't I have that?* will want to pick up this book."

—Rachel Bertsche, bestselling author of
MWF Seeking BFF: My Yearlong Search for a New Best Friend

"Shasta Nelson has put her finger on the pulse of our cultural malaise: We need good friends to have a happy life, but we are disconnected from one another. Repair takes insight, courage, and strength, and Shasta provides outstanding encouragement for us to get up, snap ourselves out of our self-defeating patterns, and create the friendships that our souls are longing for. *Frientimacy* has already changed my life, and it will change yours."

—Marilyn Paul, bestselling author of
It's Hard to Make a Difference When You Can't Find Your Keys

"If you desire friends you can count on and grow with, who will support and see you, who make your life more full and fun, then you've got to read *Frientimacy*. Shasta Nelson has taken a bold stand to end loneliness and replace it with the deep and nourishing bonds of sisterhood we all need and crave."

—Christine Arylo, bestselling author of
Madly in Love with ME and *Reform Your Inner Mean Girl*

"I used to get a terrible sinking feeling in my stomach when I read articles about how women with a close circle of friends live longer. I had such a hard time developing satisfying friendships after a certain age. I was lonely! But not anymore, and I attribute part of that ability to connect to Shasta Nelson's wisdom. If you want—and need!—deeper friendships, then please read this wise and useful book."

—Jennifer Louden, bestselling author of
The Woman's Comfort Book and *The Life Organizer*

"Compassionate and encouraging, Shasta Nelson teaches how to not only make friends but create deep connections and avoid 'expectation hangovers' in our friendships. I am so grateful for this book, and all the loving, connected, and lasting friendships it will create."

—Christine Hassler, bestselling author of
20 Something, 20 Everything

"The best friendships never have been simple. . . . Lo and behold, Shasta Nelson's gentle urgings toward self-improvement result in vastly more satisfying friendships."

—Theresa Donovan Brown, co-author of
The Social Sex: A History of Female Friendship

"Even women with large numbers of friends yearn for close, intimate friendships: Relationships that are easy and forgiving, and that allow friends to communicate in shorthand yet feel understood. In *Frientimacy*, Shasta Nelson offers practical advice to help women hone the skills and mindsets that are fundamental to the development of healthier, more satisfying friendships."

—Irene S. Levine, author of
Best Friends Forever: Surviving a Breakup with Your Best Friend

"Many women feel they have enough friends but are stuck feeling unsatisfied . . . *Frientimacy* is a thorough and indispensible guide to help understand what's missing, and learn how to take the next steps to connect in the most fulfilling ways possible."

—Andrea Bonior, PhD, author of
The Friendship Fix and
The Washington Post Express column "Baggage Check"

FRIENTIMACY

How to Deepen Friendships for Lifelong
Health and Happiness

Shasta Nelson

SEAL

Seal Press

Nelson, Shasta, author.
Frientimacy : how to deepen friendships for lifelong health and happiness / by Shasta Nelson.
Berkeley, California : Seal Press, [2016]
LCCN 2015045221 | ISBN 9781580056076 (paperback)
LCSH: Friendship. | Interpersonal relations. | BISAC: SELF-HELP / Personal Growth / General.
LCC BF575.F66 N453 2016 | DDC 155.3/3392--dc23
LC record available at http://lccn.loc.gov/2015045221

Published by

SEAL PRESS
A Member of the Perseus Books Group
1700 Fourth Street
Berkeley, California
Sealpress.com

Cover Design: Kara Davison/Faceout Studio | Interior Design: Kate Basart/Union Pageworks

Printed in the United States of America
Distributed by Publishers Group West

LSC-C

10 9 8 7 6 5 4

To the community of women in GirlFriendCircles.com: Thank you for heeding the call of your heart to be more connected to others; may you be blessed with courage as you build your frientimacy, and may you rest in trust that you are gifting the world with more love.

♥

And to my husband, Greg, whose long walks and endless talks with me not only helped me articulate what I felt called to say in this book but also whose love gave me the courage to say it.

Contents

Before you start, we have a gift for you!

Frientimacy Gift Pack

Includes:

- The Frientimacy Workbook: to help you reflect on and practice the concepts in this book.
- The Frientimacy Quiz: which you can take both before and after reading the book. Find out how much your frientimacy increases!
- Two different book club guides: Frientimacy 1X (for groups meeting once) or Frientimacy 4X (for groups meeting just once or four times).

Download your free copy at Frientimacy.com.

It seems impossible to love people who hurt and disappoint us,
yet there are no other kinds of people.

—Frank Andrews, author of *The Art and Practice of Loving*

Introduction

Chances are high that you have an intimacy gap in your life.

I'm not referring to the intimacy of a romantic relationship, but rather the lack of depth many of us feel in our friendship intimacy, or "frientimacy." That is, a gap between the kind of friendships you *want* to have and the ones you *do* have. This isn't to say your friends aren't great people, or that you're not a great friend. This is to say that, if you're like most people, something in you *knows* that you have the capacity to both give and receive far more support, love, and intimacy than you currently enjoy.

This is because we're social beings. We don't just thrive on *feeling* emotionally connected to others; research shows that we're *wired* to connect with others—that we actually function best when we feel we are woven tightly into relationships. Unfortunately, too often in this day and age we feel less connected than we'd like—no matter how many social media friends or connections we have.

Here are some ways that many women have expressed this desire:

- I am over being networked; I just want a few close friends.
- I am ready for comfortable.
- I have a social life, but that's different than feeling really connected.
- I just want to feel like I belong.
- I long for more relaxed time to connect with the people I love.
- I prefer deep.
- I want friends I believe in and admire.
- I want to feel accepted.
- I want to know that someone is there for me.
- I want to laugh and tell secrets with someone I trust.
- I wish I had a tribe.
- I'd give anything to be surrounded by friends—really, really good friends.

If just one of the lines above speaks to you, then know that what you want is very human. It's the bravest, healthiest, and most loving among us who will admit our desire for greater frientimacy. Know, too, that you're not alone. I believe we live in a world where the need is nearly universal. Our sense of disconnection is far more cultural than it is circumstantial, more widespread than it is personal.

The good news is we can work to close this gap. In so doing we will not only invite more intimacy into our lives—we will actually deepen our lives. This is because healthy, vibrant relationships help us to develop and actualize the joy, meaning, and peace that we crave.

The chapters to follow will walk you through all this and more.

- In Part 1: The Intimacy Gap, we'll discuss what it means to acknowledge and own our intimacy gaps.

- In Part 2: The Frientimacy Triangle, we'll discuss the tri-fold approach to embracing and deepening frientimacy: by enhancing the positivity, consistency, and vulnerability in all our friendships.

- In Part 3: Obstacles to Intimacy, we'll discuss the various stumbling blocks that can trip up our path to frientimacy.

- Then, in the conclusion, we'll cover how we can measure how far we've come by tracking relationship growth, courage growth, and love growth.

If you have fewer confidantes than you'd like, and less support than you need, then I welcome you to join me in learning how you can close your intimacy gap and deepen your frientimacy. In so doing you can improve your health and longevity, increase the joy you experience, add meaning to your life, and feel more loved.

But you'll be doing even more than that. I think the world is dying without the intimacy it needs. In improving your own relationships, you can also help to heal the world. Every person who feels connected and valued is more likely to share the love—and the more love in the world, the happier we all will be. Join me!

With huge love,

♡ Shasta

PART 1

The Intimacy Gap

Though many of us have friends and friendships we care about, we don't necessarily feel the depth of intimacy we'd like to feel. That yearning indicates we have an intimacy gap—which, in these times of high productivity and low free time, can result from any number of factors. In chapter 1, we'll learn the ins and outs of Acknowledging Our Intimacy Gaps for what they are—and what they aren't.

The discussion continues in chapter 2, where we'll learn about Committing to Closing our Intimacy Gaps, including any uncomfortable feelings that can emerge from self-exploration. We do this because we know that frientimacy doesn't just happen; we have to work at it. But we can also be gentle and patient with ourselves as we practice personal growth, acknowledging it will take time, just as will frientimacy itself.

Let's get started!

1

Acknowledging Our Intimacy Gaps

was about to come face-to-face with one of my intimacy gaps.

Arriving at the café to meet up with my girlfriends, all I felt was excitement. We hadn't kept up with our weekly Tuesday girls' nights over the holiday season, so we hugged like long-lost friends with a lot of catching up to do.

In an attempt to encourage more intentional sharing and deeper connection, I suggested we go around the circle, saying one thing that we appreciate about our group friendship and one thing we want more of from the group. Since two of the most important actions in strengthening friendships are to affirm what we value and to let others know what kind of support would be meaningful to us, I thought this could be a perfect way to open our New Year together.

Everyone eagerly answered the question, and the sharing felt really meaningful. I was touched to hear each person share what she'd like more of from the group, including: continued understanding for repeatedly talking about the same problem, asking for more encouragement during a particularly rough patch, even getting together *more often* than we already did.

As they talked, I was thinking ahead to what I would say. I decided to be truly honest and share that it would feel good to have them initiate asking about my life a bit more. I often did that for them but didn't feel they asked about me quite as frequently—to the extent that I sometimes left our evenings feeling we'd spent more individual time on everyone else's life than on mine.

But my turn to share never came! It was *almost* comical—right before my turn everyone got absorbed in stories prompted by the last answer. Like kids distracted by candy, the conversation ended up veering in another direction. I kept waiting for one of them to ask me to share. No one did.

On the way home I flip-flopped between licking my wounds and pretending I didn't really care. But there was no denying that I felt pity for myself, frustration toward them, and disappointment in how suddenly these friendships felt far from fulfilling.

I blamed them. *They* were clearly selfish, caught up in their own lives, and unable to fulfill my needs. A few other memories popped up with confirmation to support that I was always the one who gives, who asks, who glues us together. *I* was the amazing friend and they were the problem. The verdict felt good, so I pushed down the little voice of wisdom and responsibility that was gearing up to tone down my pity-party. She would undoubtedly speak up soon, but I wasn't ready for her yet. Instead, I just sat in the disillusionment of the intimacy gap in which I found myself. What I wanted was the gut-warming feeling of being with amazing people who loved me; what I had was that gut-wrenching feeling of being neglected.

There was a gap between the friendships I wanted and the friendships I had.

What We Have: Dissatisfaction in Our Relationships

It's not lost on me that, though I felt disappointed in my friends, in some ways I was living my dream: being with a group of local and very close friends in a café. In my first book, *Friendships Don't Just Happen*, I described standing on a sidewalk looking at a group of women laughing and talking inside a café. I had recently moved away from my good friends, so I felt like the puppy in the window hoping to be adopted, wanting to be chosen, wishing I had friends I met with regularly for meaningful sharing.

That loneliness whispering her wisdom to me on that sidewalk prompted me to start the process of making new friends in a new city. But since making close friends isn't a fast or automatic process, it would be at least a year before I could say I had friends; it took another year or two before I trusted them, confided in them, and relied on them. Most of us need six to eight times together before we start feeling a rhythm of being together—a comfortable familiarity—but it can take years before we feel we have the frientimacy—friendship intimacy—we crave.

Friendships between women get a lot of hype—from inspirational stories of people donating a kidney to a friend to the pink sparkly folklore of girls nights out and girlfriend vacations. So it's easy to think most women have an amazing tribe rich with laughter, secrets, chick flicks, and pots of proverbial soup. But the truth is that between two-thirds and three-fourths of Americans believe there is more loneliness in today's society than there used to be, report dissatisfaction in their current friendships, and feel they have fewer meaningful relationships than they did five years ago. Another statistic comes from a study, published in *American Sociological Review* that looked at two decades of social isolation in the United States. To the question of how many confidantes one has, in 1994 the common answer was two to three confidantes; as of 2004 the answer was closer to zero. I think it's safe to say that the way we're currently doing friendship isn't working for the vast majority of us.

But what about your experience? Feel free to answer the questions below. (Or you can download a copy of *The Frientimacy Workbook*, which includes all the exercises in this book. Visit www.Frientimacy.com.)

Friendship Intimacy Satisfaction Scale

How satisfied are you with your current level of frientimacy (friendship intimacy)? On a scale of 1–10, with ten representing the ideal level of frientimacy, what number would you give your current experience?

NO FULFILLMENT   IDEAL FULFILLMENT

| 1 | 2 | 3 | 4 | 5 | 6 | 7 | 8 | 9 | 10 |

What one thing comes to mind that could increase that number for you?

In of 2015, I conducted a Frientimacy Survey in which twelve hundred women rated their frientimacy satisfaction; here are their results:

10	5.7%
9	4.48%
8	10.99%
7	12.75%
6	13.16%
5	11.13%
4	8.28%
3	11.94%
2	10.45%
1	11.13%

I'm thrilled that 20 percent reported an 8 or higher. But note that most women are twice as likely to score a 1 or 2 than a 9 or 10; and that over 50 percent are at 5 or below.

And it's not just women. I believe wholeheartedly that men crave more intimacy in their relationships, too, so I strongly advocate more fulfilling relationships for both genders. Although this book was crafted to speak to women in particular, the truth is that, regardless of our gender, there is a gap between the frientimacy we have and the frientimacy we want.

But first we need to be able to identify our experience, to realize just what it is we want. And that can be hard. For example, when I'm in front of an audience, I often ask, "How many of you are lonely?" As you might imagine, the inclusion of the dreaded L word means very few hands go up, though I do see a few heads nod.

But when I ask, "Do you wish you had more deep and meaningful friendships?" nearly every hand rises.

Though we may know a lot of people, that doesn't mean we feel we have meaningful connections. But if we don't acknowledge our need—and admit that we lack meaningful connections, that we feel disconnected—we limit our chances of getting our needs met. In other words, if we don't identify the problem, we can't do anything about it. Many of us don't acknowledge our need for intimacy because we don't want to acknowledge a simple fact: that feeling disconnected is a form of loneliness.

Some would say only recluses and "loners" are truly lonely—and most people are neither. But to limit the classification of loneliness to only those whom professionals might consider chronically lonely (or even depressed) is like using the word "hungry" to describe only those dying of starvation with no access to food. Just because I'm not malnourished doesn't mean that I don't regularly feel hunger—and that certainly doesn't mean I don't need to respond to my hunger. Likewise with our loneliness: Just because we aren't extremely lonely doesn't mean we don't experience loneliness. We do, and we need to respond to it, because the reality is that many of us are far more disconnected from intimacy than we want to be.

But there's a second obstacle to address: not *wanting* to admit we're lonely. When I ask my audiences to call out what comes to their minds when they hear the word *lonely*, common responses include: *depressed, sad, isolated,* and *bitter.* Given those replies, it's no wonder we're so afraid to concede to feeling lonely. To utter the word "lonely" might reveal that something is wrong with us, that no one likes us, that we have no friends.

We're fine, we tell ourselves. We know people we *could* call. We talk to people every day, sometimes all day long! Our friends really *would* be there for us if we needed them. In fact, we're actually too busy to stay in touch more than we do now, right? We already feel guilty for not being better friends, parents, daughters, and partners. Truthfully, we have so many responsibilities that we really don't even have the time or energy to do much more than we're already doing. In fact, if given the choice between a quiet night in the bathtub with a favorite magazine versus an evening of going out, we'd prefer that quiet night— so doesn't that prove we're not lonely? Put simply, we are so resistant to the possibility that we feel lonely we can talk ourselves out of any hint of the truth.

In the wonderfully titled book *Alone Together,* author Sherry Turkle warns: "Networked, we are together, but so lessened are our expectations of each other that we can feel utterly alone. And there is the risk that we come to see each other as objects to be accessed—and only for the parts we find useful, comforting, or amusing."

Note that she said, "*feel* utterly alone."

Loneliness is subjective, and it's not the same as being alone. One can be alone and not feel lonely; we can also be surrounded by people and still feel lonely. Indeed, many of us aren't lonely because we don't know people; we're lonely because the vast majority of those relationships lack the depth and ease and intimacy that we crave. For many of us, it's not that we need to meet new people, it's that we need to know how to go deeper with the people we already know.

So I'd like to clarify what I do and don't mean when I say we're lonely.

WE'RE NOT LONELY because we don't have any friends; we're lonely because those friends don't always leave us feeling better for having spent time with them. Like me driving away from the café that day, my loneliness wasn't from lack of relationships, but from lack of feeling the attention I wanted from those relationships.

WE'RE NOT LONELY because we have nothing in our lives that matters; we're lonely because we want to share the things that matter to us with people who care about us.

WE'RE NOT LONELY because we aren't lovable; we're lonely *because* we're so lovable. We simply have room for far more affirmation, laughter, and honest conversation than we're actually getting.

WE'RE NOT LONELY from a lack of networking; we're lonely because online profiles and Facebook check-ins don't provide the deep satisfaction that we crave.

WE'RE LONELY because we want more meaningful and healthy relationships with people who love us well—what I call Commitment Friends. (For more information, see "The 5 Types of Friends" in *The Frientimacy Workbook* so you can both assess your current friendships and better understand which ones you want.)

John T. Cacioppo and William Patrick, authors of the book *Loneliness: Human Nature and the Need for Social Connection,* sum it up well: "The problems arise simply when there is a mismatch between the level of social connection desired and the level the environment provides." In other words, the sensation of loneliness is simply information that you are ready to feel more connected to others.

By my definition, the sensation of loneliness is simply information that you're ready to feel more connected to others.

How Did We Get Here?

So if we know there's a gap between the intimacy we have and the intimacy we wish we had, what's stopping us from doing something about it? Here are a few answers I've heard to this question:

- "It's because we live in a culture where no one has the time to get together anymore."
- "It's our world of social media and the impact of technology in our society."

- "It's because we live in a world where everyone is a consumer, a taker, someone who only wants friendship when it's convenient. Everyone is so toxic and narcissistic."

Answers like these suggest we're not likely to agree on what the root problem is. And though the sociologists studying shifts in relationships offer more nuanced hypotheses, they're certainly not in agreement. What is clear is that this gap is a cultural problem.

Over the last several decades there has been a steady decline in nearly all the traditional organizations that brought people together, groups like religious bodies, civic organizations, poker leagues, neighborhood associations, and bridge clubs. In the now landmark book *Bowling Alone: The Collapse and Revival of American Community,* Robert D. Putnam tries to understand the curious fact that, even though more people go bowling today than they did in the 1950s and 1960s, there are fewer bowling leagues today. He highlights how

> for the first two-thirds of the twentieth century a powerful tide bore Americans into ever deeper engagement in the lives of their communities, but a few decades ago—silently, without warning—the tide reversed and we were overtaken by a treacherous rip current. Without at first noticing, we have been pulled apart from one another and from our communities over the last third of the century.

One could argue that there are many new ways of connecting that are exciting, meaningful, and rewarding. But it'd be hard to make a case that most of us feel more supported than ever. Connected, perhaps, but not sustained. We feel like we have threads reaching out to many people, but that those very strands aren't woven together to create a net that will hold us.

Putnam reiterates that all the research reveals that

> virtually no corner of American society has been immune to the anticivic contagion. It has affected men and women; central cities, suburbs, and small towns; the wealthy, the poor, and the middle class; blacks, whites, and other ethnic groups; people who work

and those who don't; married couples and swinging singles; North, South, both coasts, and the heartland.

My personal experience backs up his findings: The disconnection we feel with our neighbors, our cities, our families, and our circles of friends is widespread—and the causes are hard to pin down. For every person who tells me their children are the reason they don't have friends, another will tell me they've found it easier to make friends now that they have kids. People from every city and town try to convince me *theirs* is the most challenging—in one locale, the rain is to blame for a dissatisfactory social life; in another, the gorgeous weather is at fault, since it encourages weekend exodus. Some areas, apparently, are just "one-mind" towns, where everyone is "too" focused on the same thing, like politics or the movie industry; while in another area, everyone is "too" different from each other to find someone with whom to connect.

And nor can we blame our personal temperament. Even the most extraverted and outgoing among us know the pain of wishing we had closer friends. Research suggests that most of us replace half our closest friends every seven years; at that rate, basically anyone experiencing life change will experience some friendship losses and transitions, many times over.

Fortunately, Robert Putnam also argues that, though history does demonstrate an overall decline in our civic engagement and social capital development over the centuries, it also demonstrates there are ebbs and flows to society's ability to connect and engage. As such, we could be on the verge of another cycle of deep and wide connecting.

The Damage of Disconnection

George Monbiot, an investigative reporter and cultural commentator, wrote in his column in *The Guardian* that loneliness is killing us. He labels this era—much as we did with the Stone Age, Iron Age, Space Age, and Information Age—the "Age of Loneliness." Research shows that feeling disconnected can be as detrimental to our bodies as addictions to alcohol or cigarettes. Much like lungs that have gone from healthy pink to eerie black, feeling like we aren't supported, known, or loved leaves its mark, too.

Physiologically, loneliness or disconnection depletes our immune systems, which in turn saps our energy. Psychologically, loneliness weakens our confidence, lowers our happiness, and nags us with anxiety. Even more unfortunate is the fact that we can live with these symptoms so regularly we come to see them as normal. But though the preceding concerns, while unpleasant, may sound survivable, think again. Rates of dementia, addiction, accidents, depression, anxiety, suicide, murder, and paranoia all can increase when emotional connections are decreased.

One study powerfully illustrated the effects of disconnection on our bodies by scanning the brain processes of women under stress. The study tracked the brain activity of women intermittently receiving mild electric shocks that stimulated (or even simulated) the stress so many of us live with every day, the stress of always anticipating life with a sense of uncertainty. The results demonstrated that the brains of women allowed to hold the hand of a friend during the procedure processed significantly lower stress levels. In other words, the parts of our brains that sense danger are much less active when we feel like we're not in it alone.

According to Dr. James Coan, the lead researcher in this study and a neuroscientist at the University of Virginia, "The burden of coping with life's many stressors . . . when you have to deal with them all by yourself not only feels more exhausting, it literally creates more wear on your body."

Of course, having friends doesn't prevent the various shocks we experience in life—life still happens—but the emotional support of intimate relationships definitively protects our bodies from the harmful results of stressful events. Our relationships thus buffer hardship, both limiting the damaging effects of those stressors and protecting us from absorbing the impact.

In research revealed in *Chasing the Scream: The First and Last Days of the War on Drugs,* Johann Hari revealed what might be one of the most shocking effects of not having a community. One study demonstrated that a caged rat, when given the choice between a bottle of water and a bottle of water laced with cocaine or heroin, always returned to the drug—until it died. This isn't too surprising; most of us believe that certain drugs are addictive. But what happened when they tested a rat that was given delicious rat food, fun toys, and plenty of friends? Not one "happy environment" rat opted for the laced bottle.

In his attempt to find out what, if anything, could really help heal an addiction, Hari concludes: "The opposite of addiction is not sobriety. It is human connection."

In other words, whenever we deny our need for deep and meaningful connection we are in truth refusing the medicine that can save us.

Worth Remembering

- Though many of us have friends and friendships we care about, we don't necessarily feel the depth of intimacy we'd like to feel.

- Most of us need six to eight times together before we start feeling a rhythm of being together and reach a comfortable familiarity. But it can take years before we might feel we have the frientimacy—friendship intimacy—that we crave.

- To realize we'd like more intimacy than we have is to acknowledge we have an intimacy gap.

- We didn't get to this point in a vacuum; there are lots of reasons why many of us feel less connected than we'd like.

- It's important to acknowledge that maintaining intimacy gaps—in essence, sustaining our sense of disconnection—damages us in the long run. One of the best things we can do for ourselves is to deepen the intimacy in our lives.

To follow we'll discuss the next step in closing our intimacy gaps: owning our gaps.

2

Committing to Closing Our Intimacy Gaps

While driving home from the afternoon where my friends neglected to ask me to share, the last thing I wanted was an invitation to admit my need and take responsibility. I had no desire to be the one to accept growth. On the contrary, what I wanted was someone to tell *them* to grow up!

But that was the problem. Standing on the edge of our gap, hoping to move toward greater intimacy, is akin to standing on a diving board for the first time. Even if we know how to swim, the leap of even one foot may as well be a black hole.

By and large, we aren't big fans of gaps. If the gap we experience is a life transition, many of us rush toward a new beginning to help get over an ending. If the gap is between our teeth, we're inclined to wire them together. If the gap is in a conversation, we find words to fill the silence. When a question is asked, we expect an answer to follow. Even the definition of a gap—a space that is unfilled—describes what is lacking rather than what is. Our brains often want to close gaps to avoid the dissonance of something feeling incomplete.

It's crucial to realize that whispering our hunger for greater connection doesn't *create* the gap. The gap is already there; we're simply now choosing the sting of honesty over the dull ache of avoidance. But the sting of honesty, while seemingly sharper, can be also short-lived because it can encourage us to take actions to transform our lives—whereas the dull ache of denial can plague us indefinitely.

Maturity, measured in part by our Emotional Intelligence (EQ), is the ability to manage our emotions in healthy ways. To transform our feelings, we have to first step out of denial and admit what they are.

The Glaring Gap Between the Friends We Have and The Friends We Want

Here is many women's fantasy of the perfect friend: she'd know exactly how to respond when we text her a code word; she'd show up with a pot of soup when she heard we were sick; she'd never complain about our ranting about X, *again*; she'd include us in everything; she'd share secrets she tells no one else; and she'd want to be with us when we want to be with her—no more, no less.

When we feel that nagging angst of loneliness, it's for *that friend* that we hanker. The fantasy best friend: the one who is the Thelma to our Louise, the laughter to our jokes, and the remedy to just about everything. She would be the finisher of our sentences, the reader of our minds, and the affirmer of our hearts. Our time together would be effortless, easy, safe, and comfortable.

Far too many of us ache for her, hoping we'll happen upon her while doing little to actually seek her out. Some of us go one step further and decide to put at least *some* energy toward the search—we join sites like www.Girl FriendCircles.com, sign up for workshops and classes, and attend the parties of our established friends with a willingness to make new friends. We go out looking for her as though we're casting agents hosting an audition.

But then, much to our dismay, we discover that the difference between what we *want* and what we *get* is vastly huge.

Because what we get in a new friend, 90 percent of the time, is a stranger we don't yet know as a best friend, so we don't yet love her. So we feel discouraged when she takes three weeks to schedule, we feel skeptical when she seems to have other friends, we feel doubtful when we see our two lives aren't as similar as we'd hoped, and we feel judgmental when we see her choose differently than we would have. She's not quite as vulnerable as we prefer, the conversation doesn't go as deep as we wish, and we're not laughing quite as much as we think we should be.

Ultimately, we meet a bunch of "candidates" who aren't quite good enough to fit our BFF opening, so we quietly reject them and keep looking, albeit while feeling somewhat disillusioned.

We don't need better friends; we need better friendships.

All of this is to say there's a myth that needs busting: that there is a "right" person to be one's BFF. Many women remain lonely because they think having close friends is a product of *discovering* the right people. But the truth is that meaningful friendship is actually the product of *developing* the right friendships. I'll repeat this because this is a truth that needs embracing: Friendships don't start with frientimacy; they are developed.

Pretend you meet me and decide you'd love to be my BFF. You'd likely have a fantasy of what it would be like to be my friend, and then as you reach out to me you'd start judging my responses against that ideal picture. You might think: "*Ugh, she already has her good friends, I doubt she has time for me . . . Plus she's so busy and I want someone who could meet up with me tonight if I wanted . . . And when I see her she just doesn't open up about her life that much . . . And I invited her last time and she hasn't reciprocated yet . . . Besides, her life really is too different from mine.*" All these sorts of interpretations of my behaviors might tempt your brain into ruling me out.

But here's the genius: As long as I'm friendly toward you—then I should meet the standards for being your new friend.

For the truth is that, if you and I barely know each other, then you shouldn't really be trying to figure out whether I could be your BFF. Instead, be excited that we're new friends! Everything I named above as reasons you might rule me out are actually appropriate and healthy actions—for that beginning level of friendship. I really shouldn't be expected to open up with you yet, to drop everything for you, or to feel pressured to invite you out in order to keep our friendship "equal." Besides, it isn't fair to judge me or guess what I'll be like as a BFF by how I treat you as a new friend. The truth is that I, appropriately, give different levels of myself to people based on the friendship that has been *developed* between us.

In other words, don't use the standards you'd have for a best friend for a new friend! For a new friendship, lower your standards appropriately.

"Lower my standards?" you might reply, panic rising in your voice.

Yes, lower your standards. Release your expectations. Stop trying to pick and choose so early in the game. As long as there are no red flags—like abusive behavior, lying, being mean-spirited—then be open to being surprised by who might develop into a meaningful friend. Basically, I can let nearly *anyone* into my "new friends" circle. As long as you're not biting me or screaming at me—then, nice to meet you!

We'd be wise to recognize that all levels of friendship are important, as well as to acknowledge that we don't always know which women will be the ones we grow closer to. Truthfully, my best friends aren't necessarily the women I liked more than anyone else I knew at the time—they are simply the ones with whom the relationship continued to develop.

Frientimacy takes time.

The Truth About Gaps

To follow are two truths I've learned over the years as I've lived through my own gaps: It's in gaps where we grow, and closing gaps can be scary.

Growth Begins in the Gaps

We experience cognitive dissonance, the recognition that something feels unresolved or out of alignment, during the intervals of life where we'd rather be *in* something than left in limbo. It's the land of the in-between, and many of us resist it if we can.

But it's in realizing that we don't have what we want—or that we don't want something we have—that encourages us to seek out what we *do* want. No one starts a diet, quits a job, or takes a risk of any kind without first feeling the gap between the current and preferred scenario. If we are willing to admit feeling hungry for greater connection, then we're better able to choose the actions that will lead to more meaningful friendships. So, ultimately and ideally, our gaps invite our growth.

Fortunately, simply acknowledging we have a gap can generate the energy needed to effect change. Sometimes just the act of admitting we want more intimacy can bring us the impetus to carve a new path—giving us, for example, the eyes to see opportunities we never noticed before, the courage to say "yes" instead of going home as usual, or the conviction to have the awkward conversation we'd normally put off. And that new energy is essential: If we don't want to live our whole lives feeling disconnected, we have to be willing to show up with a new approach. And in order to do that, we have to visualize our goal.

Brain imaging studies have repeatedly demonstrated how the same parts of the brain fire whether we're only imagining an activity or actually doing it. That's why scary movies can be so exhilarating, and how athletes can improve their performance as much from imaginary practice sessions as from actual practice. And that's why setting goals matters: If we can imagine it, then the chances that we can, in fact, do it go up exponentially. Thinking, writing, or speaking about what we want stimulates the brain activity that gives us the energy and motivation to move forward.

The trick is, change can be scary. So it's important to remind ourselves that 1) it's normal to feel uncertain about effecting change, and 2) we can't let our fears hinder our progress.

Why? Because we can't remain in the gap indefinitely; it's too demoralizing to not see the distance between here and there eventually closing. So there are only two paths out of the dissonance—changing our lives, or changing our desires—and eventually we must choose. If we keep saying something is important to us but then do nothing about it, we will ultimately lose both our trust in ourselves and our sense of integrity, not to mention that we'll never get to our preferred future.

But to get from Point A to Point B we have to take the first step. Point B isn't coming to us: Intimacy won't come knocking on our door, gifting itself with a red bow. So, to get started, let's imagine different scenarios of steps we might take—and, most important, imagine surviving their results:

- We will take a tentative step forward. It'll be disorienting, not because it's wrong or bad, but just because it's new. We'll initiate with someone and feel scared. That fear doesn't mean we shouldn't have initiated—it only means we're not used to it.

- We'll share openly but then feel like we have a vulnerability hangover the next day. That's okay. It doesn't mean we should never share again—it just means we need to pace ourselves.

- Someone asks us to forgive and we freak out, every fiber of our bodies crying out for revenge. That panic doesn't signal that forgiveness is the wrong path—it just signals that your forgiveness muscle is underpracticed.

- We're offered a compliment that we're tempted to brush off, but instead we stammer a "thank-you," trusting that over time it will get easier to receive what right now can feel uncomfortable.

- We feel envy when someone gets what we want, but we congratulate her anyway, remembering that begrudging someone else has never brought us peace.

In other words, we are going to try new things, and we should expect them to feel disorienting. We understand that to get in emotional shape for intimacy we will have to exercise muscles we didn't know we had. We'll be sore. There will be times when we won't know if it's working or if we're doing it right. But we won't retreat just because it's new and unfamiliar. In fact, we will *expect* it to be new and unfamiliar—because we can't get *there* and stay *here* at the same time.

When we feel a lack of intimacy, the first thing to explore is ourselves.

Intimacy as Exercise

So, how do we go about bringing our best self to our relationships? We work at it. The trick is to stick with it, with realistic expectations of how our progress will unfold. And one of the best ways to do that is to think of relationship work as just another form of exercise that we do to keep healthy.

Exercise is a good metaphor for intimacy because most of us know that, to become healthier, we will sometimes feel and look worse before we feel and look better. Our muscles have to be stretched and strained a bit before they can become stronger; our skin must sweat out the heat to keep our body regulated. We go in expecting exhaustion and discomfort—even wanting it!—as proof of our exertion.

The same is true for relationships. Far too many of us seem to think that intimacy should come without sweat, effort, or ache. When another person disappoints us, we sometimes withdraw, emotionally gun-shy. When we feel a pit in our stomachs or an ache in our hearts, we can be quick to toss around labels like "toxic" or "unhealthy," and can assume that our best option is avoidance.

I invite you to not avoid your emotional sweat, and to not avoid your relational sweat.

To return briefly to the afternoon with my friends at the café where I felt left out: I was definitely tempted to cut my losses. One voice in my head—who fancies herself an idealist, convinced perfection *is* out there—wanted me to walk away with my head held high, convinced they weren't good enough friends for me. Another voice, let's call her my lazy side, was exhausted by just the idea of starting over with new friends—not to mention the awkwardness of ending these friendships, especially since my lazy side avoids conflict at every possible turn. That side of me moped: "Oh please just put up with it. You enjoy them most of the time. You can't expect everyone to live up to your standards!" So, put all together, the idealist voice insisted that following her path would ensure I was a strong woman, while the lazy voice compelled me to be a compassionate woman. But that wasn't a choice I was willing to make—I wanted to be both.

We might all express those two paths differently based on our temperaments and personalities, but when we're under stress—which disappointment and frustration certainly fall under—our human temptation is to fight or to flee, to go big or to go home. (In fact, this is such a common response that the phenomenon has been phrased in umpteen ways: Bark vs. play dead. Be aggressive vs. acquiesce. Go it alone in independence vs. cling in codependence. Assert vs. withdraw. "Don't settle" vs. "Be Content." Retaliate vs. swallow it. Make a scene vs. stay silent. Fists up vs. walk away. Hold your ground vs. lie low as a doormat. "It's all *their* fault" vs. "It's all *our* fault." Puff big vs. shrink small.)

Since most of us tend to avoid conflict, especially with our friends, a large majority of us choose a combination of the two. First we put up with it for as long as we can; after that, we make up excuses and slowly drift apart.

Intimacy requires a third path: lean in.

If Ms. Fight rushes in with loud declaration, and Ms. Flight slinks back in resignation, then Ms. Lean In takes one step closer in hopes of mending and improving the connection. Leaning in acknowledges that we're still figuring it out, that we're bound to all behave imperfectly some of the time, and that we can practice love far more easily when we're open and present than when we've turned our backs.

Pay special attention to the phrasing "still figuring it out." Much the way we can't expect to run a marathon if we haven't been in training, we can't expect to maturely respond in every relationship circumstance if we haven't yet practiced much. Every trade and talent requires practice to improve; intimacy is no different. We *become* people who foster intimacy—we develop *into* those who choose to engage and connect with others. And we must practice to get there. So if I wanted to be both the strong-woman idealist who is also compassionate, I didn't have to choose one over the other; I just had to practice being both.

Our Responsibility in the Gap

Once we set out to take those first steps, we need to keep something in mind: When we feel a lack of intimacy, the first thing to explore is ourselves. What do I mean by this?

I'm often approached by women who feel slighted, misunderstood, frustrated, or taken for granted by their friends. One friend doesn't understand what it's like to be a mom, another talks too much about herself; one won't make time to get together for more than a quick lunch here and there, another never reciprocates invitations; one friend is having an affair, and another is jealous of her friend's success.

These are understandable frustrations. It's definitely easier to identify what bothers us about others, and wish they'd change, than it is to consider ourselves, isnt' it? But we can explore these feelings, asking ourselves: "*Why* does this bother me? Does it have to? How can I approach this differently? What might I be contributing to the frustration in our friendship?"

In his book *Relationship Rescue: A Seven-Step Strategy for Reconnecting with Your Partner*, TV superstar and psychologist Dr. Phil McGraw goes so far as to say, "If you are living in a dysfunctional relationship with another person, it's because you have a dysfunctional relationship with yourself." This doesn't mean *we* are dysfunctional; this only speaks to dysfunction in the *relationship*.

And the *only* way to address dysfunction in the relationship is to address the role we play in it and the actions we choose to take in relation to the other. We cannot address dysfunction by trying to change the other person. There are always *three* entities in every relationship: 1) you, 2) me, and

3) us. I'm in charge of only my part; you're in charge of only your part; and we both are in charge of what we share. If there is a problem, I create change only when I decide to work on me—and then practice showing up differently to the part that we share.

You, Me, and Us

Donald Miller in his book *Scary Close: Dropping the Act and Finding True Intimacy* shares a metaphor he learned in a group therapy session. The therapist placed three pillows on the floor, asking Donald and another person to stand on the pillows on each end, leaving the middle one vacant. Pointing to his pillow, she said, "Don, that's your pillow, that's your life. The only person who gets to step on that pillow is you. Nobody else. That's your territory, your soul." She repeated the same wisdom of owning one's space to the person standing on the other pillow.

The middle pillow, then, symbolized their relationship. Here's what Don said happened next:

"She said both of us could step into the middle pillow anytime we wanted because we'd agreed to be in a relationship. However, . . . at no point is it appropriate to step on the other person's pillow. What goes on in the other person's soul is none of your business. All you're responsible for is your own soul, nobody else's. Regarding the middle pillow, the question to ask is, "What do I want in a relationship?" If the pillow you two step on together works, that's great. If not, move on or simply explain what you'd like life to feel like in the middle pillow and see if the other person wants that kind of relationship, too. But never . . . try to change each other. Know who you are and know what you want in a relationship, and give people the freedom to be themselves."

We Are In Charge of our Happiness

I approached my second marriage with a deep and tested love in my heart but far fewer stars in my eyes. Instead of believing it was our job to make each other happy, Greg and I affirmed we'd take responsibility for our own happiness so we could bring our best selves to our relationship.

That paradigm shift expanded me and excited me. I knew that if I kept my commitment to my own personal, physical, spiritual, and emotional growth, then I'd be happier and more energized in the relationship. What I didn't know then was how self-worth fosters love for others. The more joy I fostered in my heart, the more I had to share in my relationships. And the more self-aware I was of my triggers, insecurities, superpowers, and preferences, the more I could contribute to the health of my shared relationships.

We all need others to see us and affirm us—I certainly do. But it's my job to be the sort of person who can receive others' love and attention, and that means knowing I'm worthy of their attention.

It's a bit like having a bucket that I want to keep full of love. I welcome and need others to pour their love into me, and I in turn pour my love into them. But at the end of the day, if *my* bucket is leaking, then it's not *their* job to love me more; it's *my* job to fix the leaks so I can hold what they give me. If my wounds, my needs, my insecurities, my fears—my unexamined life— have worn holes in my relationship bucket, then all the love being poured in will leak out sooner or later. Or worse, if my bucket is particularly worn, that love might never get retained at all—like water poured through a sieve.

When we believe it's the job of others to make us feel loved and worthy— be they parents, spouses, bosses, or friends—then we buy into one of the most damaging myths ever: that we're only as lovable as someone else makes us feel. There are many risks to this view. Particularly potent is how, on the one hand, we might blame others and hold them responsible for how we feel and yet, on the other hand, judge ourselves so harshly we'll do almost anything to earn affection.

But there is an alternative option. We can know our value so deeply that we're willing to admit we have room to grow—without feeling bad. It's been said that one of the most powerful statements we can make is "Maybe you're right." When we realize that our worth isn't attached one iota to being right, we can wake up to who we really are. And the path we find when we wake up can lead us to peace, love, and a desire to keep growing.

> *My wounds, needs, insecurities, and fears can wear holes*
> *in my relationship bucket. If my bucket is leaking, it's my*
> *job to fix the leaks—so I can hold the love I'm given.*

Gently Practicing Personal Growth

My own growth, spread out over a year or two, looked something like this:

1. I don't do that [*insert negative response*], nope, not me.

2. Well, maybe I do sometimes, but not as much as most people.

3. *Hmmm . . .* I just did it. Weird.

4. Well, okay, maybe I do it sometimes, but that's because it's necessary. [*Insert strong defense.*]

5. Wow I did it again . . . what is that about?!? Crazy! I could have sworn I was healthier than this.

6. Okay, I can see that I do tend to react this way when [*insert negative scenario*] happens.

7. What am I most afraid of in those moments? What am I defending against?

8. Ah-ha! Now I know why I do that. It's because I feel [*insert feeling*] when this scenario happens.

9. I wonder if I could change that response? Probably not. I mean, it's just how I'm wired. We all have our coping mechanisms and flaws, and this is mine. And it's not really that bad. It's not like I'm throwing plates at anyone, I'm just [*insert negative response*].

10. I just reacted the old way again.

11. I just reacted the old way again. [*Repeat for a few months.*]

12. You know what . . . I bet I could choose differently. It's not like I need to feel [Y] every time she does [X].

13. I'm going to change! Watch me! I'm not going to be like that anymore! I'm enlightened!

14. [X] happened, and I reacted the old way again . . .

15. . . . and beat myself up for it.

16. [X] happened, and I reacted the old way, again. It's okay . . . at least I now notice when I do it!

17. [X] happened. I caught myself in the moment—ooooh I can choose differently . . .

18. . . . but habits are hard to break, and it feels so good to defend! So I reacted the old way.

19. I'm excited that I saw I had another choice. I didn't take it because I'm so used to responding the old way, but at least I saw that I have a choice.

20. [X] happened. Caught myself in the moment. Got on a different train by responding differently. Ooooh . . . Look at the scenery—I've never been here before. I wonder where this reaction will take us?

21. She said WHAT??

22. [X] happened. Jumped off the new train, jonesing to react the old way.

23. Well . . . at least I initially chose to get on a different train. Next time I'll try to remain nondefensive instead of just delaying my reaction. But that was still good—I proved I can do it!

And so it went. Lots of hiccups, lots of fresh starts. But with time and practice and perseverance, eventually I learned to automatically choose a response derived from compassion and nondefensiveness—which opened up opportunities for greater intimacy.

It really comes down to this simple yet powerful vow: "I will take responsibility for bringing my best self to this relationship." With that we have the power to change our relationships.

My Choice to Build Frientimacy

Let's return to the anecdote of my friends with whom I hadn't been able to share my New Year wishes. While driving home, even though I couldn't wait to tell my husband how wronged I'd been, I kept hearing the little voice of maturity trying to get my attention.

I admit I'm still known for resisting her at times, but in recent years I've done my very best to give her permission to speak frankly to me. The Spirit of Conviction has proven repeatedly that, when I heed it, my life experiences more peace and joy—even if the next step isn't what I think I want. So I let her speak:

> "Shasta, you know they love you and care about your life. No one is maliciously trying to ignore you. You're making this way bigger than it needs to be. They would feel horrible if they knew they hurt you.

> "Besides, you could have handled it differently, too."

Seriously??? *I* could have responded differently? You've got to be kidding me.

> "You could have said, 'Hey before we talk about X, let's finish our sharing first.' Or, 'Before we go, I wanted to make sure I was able to tell you guys about what you mean to me . . .' And, deep inside, you know they would have loved to hear you—and then you'd be driving home feeling grateful for the friends in your life instead of licking imaginary wounds."

Imaginary? I don't think so! Just wait until I remind you of everything I've done for them and how good I am!

> "Not imaginary because they don't count. Your need to be in friendships where you feel heard is super important, and I'm so glad you can articulate that. But it's your job to ask for what you need. And honestly, to have the chance to share about your life doesn't require them to ask about it—it only requires that they receive it when you decide to share."

Ugh. By the time I got home I knew I could have handled the situation in a way that would have easily benefited all of us far more than what I actually did, sitting there quietly as though I were testing them.

Friendship doesn't mean we don't disappoint each other sometimes. It means we're in relationships where we can trust each other to speak our needs—and I hadn't done that.

It's like I believed that since they didn't prompt my sharing somehow it meant their interest wouldn't be genuine. I had attached a meaning to their actions: They care about me *if* they ask about my life, and since they didn't ask . . .

But that type of thinking is an illusion. Yes, I *feel* that way—but that doesn't make it true. Consider the same almighty feeling in a romantic relationship: "If you loved me then you wouldn't _____." We then fill in the blank with whatever we've decided indicates that our lover has chosen something over us.

In our friendships, though we probably aren't as blatant as this, and would be less likely to throw down that gauntlet when we're disappointed, we can be left with similar feelings. For example:

- "If she really cared about me then she would have called me to see how that event went."
- "If she really liked me she would have invited me to that event I saw on Facebook."
- "If she really understood my financial situation she wouldn't be asking me out for dinner at an expensive place."
- "If she really valued our friendship then she wouldn't have ignored me when she started dating."
- "If she really were a good friend then she wouldn't always try to one-up me or interrupt me when I'm talking."
- "If she really were sensitive to me being a mom she wouldn't have planned an adult-only party."
- "If she really were someone I could count on then she'd show up on time and stop canceling."

And the one most relevant to me at the time:

- "If they weren't so self-obsessed then they'd see how they didn't ask me about my life."

Indeed, it's rarely the behavior that upsets us as much as the meaning we attach to it. And since we know *our motivations* were good, then it must be that it's our friend's motivations that weren't. Yes, it feels justified; yes, it feels true—but we give up power when we make it all their fault. But we can choose to see it differently. We can practice responding in new ways.

We all have the capability of examining our own thoughts and narratives about our relationships. Many spiritual teachers attest that the greatest miracles in life aren't when circumstances change, but when thoughts change. And though we might hope that others will change their behavior, *we* are in charge of how we interpret their behavior.

For any gap in frientimacy we feel, it's easy to seem like it's *their* fault because we're so clear on what *they* could have done differently. But frientimacy doesn't build from a place of blame or apathy. Frientimacy builds when we decide to lean in. And how do we do that? Read on!

Worth Remembering

- It's important to realize that acknowledging our hunger for greater connection doesn't create an intimacy gap—it only identifies what already existed.

- Acknowledging our gaps creates energy, providing the impetus to make meaningful changes.

- In imagining our preferred future, our brains can map out the strategies to lead us to the destination we desire.

- We can expect that making changes will trigger insecurities, but that's all part of the process.

- It's important that we take responsibility for what we bring to each relationship, and know it's not another's job to make us feel loved. Love starts with us.

- We can be gentle and patient with ourselves as we practice personal growth, acknowledging it will take time.

- It's a myth that there is a "right" person to be one's BFF. And it's a truth that friendships don't start with frientimacy; they are developed.

- Frientimacy doesn't just happen; we have to work at it.

Next up: the Frientimacy Triangle—the path to intimacy.

PART 2

The Frientimacy Triangle

And now I get to share the Frientimacy Triangle with you! The Frientimacy Triangle doesn't just define what we're hoping to experience; it's also a road map of how to get there.

Chapter 3: The Way to Intimacy, provides an overview of the triangle so you can see how it all works—building the foundation before drilling deeper in the chapters that follow. We can then apply that understanding in Chapter 4: Identifying the 5 Intimacy Gaps, when we'll consider what gaps we might have in our relationships—essentially, to see why some friendships might not feel like they're working.

From there we'll discuss each side of the triangle including the most common friendship complaints within each:

- Chapter 5: Positivity: Giving *and* Receiving
- Chapter 6: Consistency: Building Trust
- Chapter 7: Vulnerability: Deepening Meaning

Altogether, you'll find numerous means of pursuing healthy relationships.

Many women have found this model incredibly helpful—and I'm so glad to be able to share it with you. Let's proceed!

3

The Way to Intimacy: The Frientimacy Triangle

The film *Avatar* tells a story of humans trying to take over the moon Pandora, where a tribe of tall, blue creatures known as the Na'vi live in harmony with nature. In the guise of a Na'vi, human Jake Sully infiltrates the community on a reconnaissance mission, during which time he falls in love with one of their warrior women, Neytiri. But theirs is more than your standard cinematic romance; I see in it an excellent depiction of what we yearn for in relationships. One line particularly struck a chord for me: "I see you."

These words, like drops of rain on a parched desert floor, are the words we all want to hear: We are seen and we matter. We are accepted and wanted. We belong. That is the result of intimacy.

What is Frientimacy?

Typically when we speak of intimacy—often referred to as the closeness between two people—we think of romantic intimacy, and even more narrowly sexual intimacy. But to reduce the entirety that is intimacy to just a sexual definition essentially leaves it stripped and naked in the bedroom. Why? Because limiting the definition to only certain acts with one person fails to even begin to fill the capacity for intimacy that most of us have. We are wired to connect with one another, and yet far too many of us have cavernous love tanks running on near empty. I most definitely want romantic intimacy for you, but far more than that singular relationship, I want you to feel deeply connected, and seen by as many people as feels right for you.

The word "intimacy" comes from the Latin *intimus,* innermost. So to be intimate merely means to share our innermost selves, which I believe can happen more wholly when we are willing to be seen by more than just one person. So while all of the principles in this book can certainly be applied to romantic relationships, I will be using the term "frientimacy"—friendship intimacy—to remind us that the intimacy we crave needn't be constrained to the realm of romance.

But before we get too technical, let's make sure we can imagine it and feel it.

Frientimacy is knowing you can call someone for any reason at all, or for no reason at all—even to just say, "I only have five minutes but I wanted to say hi!"—because you feel safe in assuming the friend will be happy to hear from you. And when you call with the biggest news, it's knowing you can share whatever you're feeling, be it elation, grief, or anything in between.

Frientimacy is sitting in your living room with girlfriends, unfiltered in your sharing. Not worrying about how you sound, what they think of you, or whether it's all coming out right the first time. Frientimacy is trusting them completely, resting in the fact that, no matter what you're sharing, you know exactly what they think of you—they admire you and love you. You know they'll strive to hear and understand you, and they won't hold anything you say against you.

Frientimacy is feeling comfortable to invite your friend to go to anything with you—whether it's a night out, a wedding you don't want to go to alone, a business event, or a two-week trip to Europe. You know your friend will appreciate the invitation, trusting that it came from a sincere place. You're also comfortable in knowing that she'll say "no" if she needs to, and that neither of you will take that personally. Frientimacy is the safety you've built together, knowing you can trust each other for an honest reply without it reflecting on the relationship.

Frientimacy is knowing whose name to put as an emergency contact, whom we can call if we're in trouble, and who would drop life to show up if we sent out an SOS signal. It's living without worrying about whether we have support. With close friends, we know we have that safety net. It's already been proven, if not yet in big ways, then at least in lots of little ways. We've been practicing with each other—showing up for births, deaths, moves, losses, weddings, and divorces.

Frientimacy is being excited to share the good news—the promotion, the decision, the pay raise, the proposal, the new opportunity. We know deeply that even if the news triggers some emotion in our friends—perhaps jealousy, competition, or sadness that we're moving away—they nonetheless take pleasure in seeing us happy. We can trust them to work through their own feelings and still cheer with us and for us.

Frientimacy isn't the goal with all our friends, but it most certainly is the goal, over time, with a few of our friends. Overall, most of us need two things: far more moments of intimacy with many people, and more consistent intimacy with a few people. Deep down, we want to be seen, connected, and accepted by many—and we can be.

Simply stated, frientimacy is any relationship where two people feel really *seen* in a way that feels *satisfying* and *safe* for both of them.

So how can we find frientimacy?

- For us to feel SATISFIED, we must feel our interaction is rewarding, practicing POSITIVITY with each other.

- For us to feel SAFE, we must feel some level of trust, practicing CONSISTENCY with each other.
- For us to feel SEEN, we must be willing to reveal ourselves, practicing being VULNERABLE with each other.

The Three Requirements of Frientimacy

To initiate, cultivate, and safeguard our intimacy, we must practice three things: positivity, consistency, and vulnerability. To follow we'll introduce each in turn, illustrate how they all work together to form the intimacy triangle, and then discuss each quality more thoroughly in chapters 5, 6, and 7.

Frientimacy = positivity + consistency + vulnerability

Frientimacy Requirement #1: Positivity

←- - - - - -→

Positivity Base

To be healthy, a friendship must start with a foundation of positivity. The more we practice it, the stronger it becomes.

I often ask crowds of women, "How many of you wish you had more significant friendships?" The invariable response is a sea of raised hands. But to my follow-up question, "And how many of you want those friends to be whiny, needy, and crying on your shoulder every time you're with them?," every hand drops.

Positivity is at the base of the triangle because a relationship cannot start or grow without it. It is highly unlikely that we'll want to reengage with friends if the last time we saw them left us feeling blamed, judged, uninterested, or exhausted.

No one who isn't codependent—and I mean no one—wants more demands, more guilt for not doing enough, more frustration, more complaints, more bitterness. No one seeks a friend who is always in crisis, suffering from heartache and needing support, awash with hardship, insecurities, and pent-up anger. We may feel compassion for them, but we won't be rushing to spend time with them.

But that said, equally significant is the fact that positivity isn't just the absence of negativity, which pokes holes in our foundation. Rather, positivity includes all the moments that strengthen and bolster our foundation: We want joy, not drama; we want laughter, not grievance; we want affirmation, not advice.

Our goal isn't to avoid all negative feelings in our lives; that's impossible. Pain, disappointment, sorrow, and frustration are all part of what it means to be human, so they'll be a part of our relationship experience, too.

Our goal then is to have a relationship where the positivity outweighs the negativity. That tipping point, according to John Gottman, is 5:1. Which means that for every stressor, heartache, or unmet expectation, our relationships need at least five positive experiences to return us to our previous equilibrium. Relationships that drop below that 5:1 ratio will erode and eventually collapse, while relationships with a high joy:pain ratio will flourish.

It's that easy. That means I can "cry on someone's shoulder" when I've deposited enough joy in our relationship account to make a withdrawal. It means we can put up with someone being late if the payoff in positivity is high. It means we can have tough conversations if we have a history of love to support them. It means we can disappoint each other on occasion—which of course we'll inevitably do—and not lose the relationship *if* we have come through for each other more often than not.

So what is positivity? I devoted an entire chapter to it in *Friendships Don't Just Happen*. In general, positivity is anything that produces a positive feeling—something that feels rewarding or satisfying. More specifically, Barbara Fredrickson, foremost expert on the subject and the author of *Positivity: Groundbreaking Research Reveals How to Embrace the Hidden Strength of Positive Emotions, Overcome Negativity, and Thrive*, notes the following ten feelings are ideal pathways to positivity: amusement, awe, gratitude, hope, inspiration, interest, joy, love, pride, and serenity.

Therefore, when we're in a new relationship our primary job should be gifting it with as many of these experiences as possible: expressing our gratitude, encouraging our friend to feel proud of her accomplishments, inviting her to inspiring events we can experience together, extending interest in her life, and ensuring our time spent together is fun. Every time we ask about someone in her life, remember her birthday, leave a comment on her Facebook post, or text a photo from our time together—we increase the positivity in our relationship.

Positive psychologist Barbara Fredrickson cites the following ten feelings as ideal pathways to positivity: amusement, awe, gratitude, hope, inspiration, interest, joy, love, pride, and serenity.

As we grow toward frientimacy, our positivity can practice expanding into bigger expressions of love: making memories on a girls' overnight getaway, speaking highly of the people she loves, helping her husband plan her surprise birthday party, calling her on Valentine's Day, and taking her to lunch to celebrate her latest victory.

Positivity in action can be different for everyone. One woman shared that she "cannot be friends with someone who doesn't make [her] laugh." Another said, "My love language is words of affirmation—if they can't cheer for me and tell me they're proud of me, we probably won't ever grow too close."

The flip side of this is captured by a woman who describes a relationship that is draining her: "Every time I leave her house I feel judged. She thinks I need to leave my marriage and change jobs and I feel like she spends her whole night trying to advise me on the life she thinks I should be living instead of asking me what I want or need. I've cried on the way home the last few times. I know she loves me but I hate who I am when I'm with her."

Without positivity as a strong foundation, a friendship does not exist.

Without positivity, the other two requirements of a friendship—consistency and vulnerability—can quickly drain one or both people. Sometimes we *choose* to remain in such relationships even when we know they drain us—perhaps because they're our relations, or coworkers, or because we want to be of service to them, or to play a certain role in their lives—but we need to remain clear that such relationships aren't *friendships*. (And, note that we're not required to remain in draining relationships for reasons of guilt, obligation, low self-esteem, or habit.)

On the other hand, we rarely want to end relationships when positivity is abundant. So the foundation of our Frientimacy Triangle is built on positivity—it's how we'll decide whom to spend more time with, why it will feel worth the effort, and how each relationship enhances our lives.

But even when we have positivity aplenty, if we rarely see each other to shore up our history and commitment, then we'll never feel truly supported. *Consistency* in a friendship is the container that holds the water for which we thirst.

Frientimacy Requirement #2: Consistency

Many of us have met women we like and admire but don't really know beyond seeing each other occasionally, often just at events. But it isn't from a lack of interest that we can't call those women our friends; it's from a lack of spending time together—a lack of consistency. We've likely met at least one person who, with enough time together, could have potentially grown into a close friend. That's because friendship has far less to do with *discovering* each other and far more to do with *developing* the relationship. And to develop something implies a process, which implies time, which implies priority, which implies commitment—which implies some level of consistency.

Consistency speaks to both the regularity and predictability necessary for two people to develop trust in each other. Without a sense of growing commitment, shown in different ways on a reoccurring basis, we won't establish the confidence in our friendship that frientimacy necessitates. When you spend more consistent time together you can begin to feel safe in guessing how your friend will respond in various situations. All this builds a level of commitment. All relationships need this temporal perspective—providing not only the confidence that our past interactions have proven meaningful but also the belief that our imagined future will continue to be so.

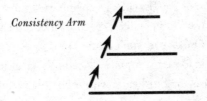

Consistency Arm

From the base of positivity we start growing the consistency arm up the left side of the triangle. As our time together increases trust and builds history, the arm extends farther up.

Starting at the base of the Triangle: When we first meet someone, our commitment to each other is simply to keep our attention on each other for the length of time we're together. So if one person is talking and the other keeps checking her phone or looking around the room, the implied commitment of paying attention isn't being honored, and so a relationship would be hard to develop from there.

Extending the consistency arm up the Triangle: As we get to know each other better, the left arm extends as the consistency increases. This can happen when, say, we follow through with an invitation after saying "we should get together sometime." Another example is honoring our time together—without canceling or postponing. Showing up when we say we will is one of the earliest and more foundational ways of building trust. Commitment means we prioritize our time together, even when we're tired, tempted to hide under the covers, or when something better comes along.

Without commitment, even if the relationship has a high positivity ratio, it ultimately wouldn't feel safe because we won't know if we can trust our friend to make time for us. We'd be scared to reach out for fear of intruding, not knowing if our invitation would be welcome. So we wouldn't be sure she'd want to fly to our wedding or host our retirement party, we'd agonize over asking for help with our new baby, and we'd take it personally if she didn't return our phone call or email. To not build up that track record of reliability leaves us feeling unsure if we really matter, and insecure about whether we really have a supportive friend when we need one.

Reaching the top of the Triangle: By the time we reach the upper part of the triangle—which we'd most likely reach with only a few people, over an extended period of time—we won't doubt how much we matter to them or how much they'd do for us in our time of need. We'd feel comfortable calling each other, even trusting our hearts with each other, confident our shared history implies a future together. Having practiced many smaller commitments, we've incrementally increased our consistency such that making the next big commitment wouldn't seem all that big. In fact, it would be an honor. We *want* to be there for our closest friends—just as we want them to be there for us.

Frientimacy Requirement #3: Vulnerability

The topic of vulnerability is all the rage right now: Articles abound, speakers pontificate, books extol. Many experts advocate being more vulnerable: less concerned with image, pretense, and hiding our shame, and more willing to be authentic, exposed, and honest about our flaws. But for all this discussion, vulnerability is nonetheless still grossly misunderstood.

Many associate vulnerability with revealing our shame—that spilling a few secrets or dragging out a skeleton or two constitutes practicing vulnerability. But revealing our shame is only one of five powerful acts of vulnerability we can practice. (We'll discuss these at length in chapter 7.)

In general terms, vulnerability does imply a sense of risk, exposure, or fear. Since none of us wants to be perceived as needy, uncertain, insecure, or defenseless, it's no wonder why we'd be reluctant to feel vulnerable, let alone venture into vulnerable territory.

But when we talk about vulnerability in a relationship we're not saying someone is defenseless because she is weak—we're saying she chooses to lower her defenses precisely because she's *not* weak. In fact, vulnerability rises from a place of safety and strength. It's a powerful act that communicates freedom. In healthy relationships we aren't forced or pressured into defenselessness; rather, we give up our defenses to each other, trusting we don't need such protection. In lowering our shields, we say to the other, "I'm here to connect, not to fight."

One of my friends describes vulnerability as the willingness to let someone else impact us. Indeed, vulnerability is a willingness to be touched or moved by others, to allow their lives to intertwine with ours—with all the attendant emotions of joy and positivity, pain and suffering as that implies. Vulnerability is anything that makes us feel we put ourselves "out there," as well as anything that "lets them in."

Now, we've doubtless all been hurt by relationships in our past, and so many feel reluctant to chance that sort of pain again. But using fear of hurt as a reason to withhold our hearts is much like deciding to not exercise again after being injured. We know it's not that *all* exercise is bad, but rather that we need to exercise differently to reduce our risk of injury. But still, no matter how perfectly we train, we know we will get injured at some point. So we rest, recover, and heal—then look for ways to not repeat the injury when we exercise again. This approach is as true of pursuing and maintaining healthy emotional activity as it is of pursuing and maintaining healthy physical activity.

To help you forge the strongest relationships you can, I'm asking you to be daring in how you offer your vulnerability. But we must also be strategic and thoughtful, ensuring we reveal, share, risk, and disclose in healthy and appropriate ways. And we do that by understanding how vulnerability works in conjunction with positivity and commitment within the Frientimacy Triangle.

Vulnerability Arm

From the base of positivity we start growing the vulnerability arm up the right side of the triangle. As our sharing increases trust and builds history, the arm extends further up.

Starting at the base of the Triangle: When we first meet someone, our vulnerability with each other could be, and in some ways "should" be, somewhat limited. A woeful or "afflicted" type who shares too much too soon often decreases her chances of developing the very intimacy she craves.

Extending the consistency arm up the Triangle: As we get to know each other better, the right arm extends as the vulnerability increases. This can happen when we've begun, say, incrementally sharing some of our more personal or private views, such as our political leanings or our faith. In deepening vulnerability, we might share past hardships or difficult decisions we've faced—and how we fared from the choices we made. In time, we can each learn to trust that the other considers our sharing a gift, one not to be casually repeated to others.

Reaching the top of the triangle: By the time we reach the upper part of the triangle—which, again, we'd most likely reach with only a few people, over an extended period of time—we won't doubt whether our secrets and deepest feelings are safe with our friend. We'd also trust that we can confide new challenges we encounter, even allowing our friend to witness new decisions to be made. Having practiced many smaller commitments, we've incrementally increased our vulnerability such that making the next disclosure wouldn't seem overwhelming. In fact, it would be an honor. Just as with consistency, we _want_ to be there for our closest friends; we care for them just as we want them to care for us.

How the Frientimacy Triangle Works

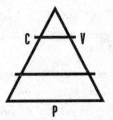

Frientimacy Triangle

The three requirements of frientimacy: **P***ositivity,* **C***onsistency, and* **V***ulnerability.*

The Frientimacy Triangle visually represents the three requirements of a healthy mutual friendship: positivity, consistency, and vulnerability. Each element is so integral to the whole that without one of these qualities a friendship does not exist.

Why is that? A brand-new friendship can't leave the station without seeing that all three tracks are in the process of being laid. Similarly, the friendship can't pull into the final destination if both people don't stay on the train. To be clear, these three elements of frientimacy are the required way stations, the map for the path, and the enjoyment of the journey. They can start, enhance, and fix any relationship.

Frientimacy then is both the peak of the mountain and the view along the way, something we can soak up and appreciate en route. We practice frientimacy knowing that, while it's a level of highest trust with another, it's also rarely an unchanging and perfect destination. Frientimacy, like intimacy, isn't a stagnant condition, a Promised Land where we can kick up our feet on arrival. Frientimacy is rather a dynamic process, one that continually invites us to enjoy the scenery. And while, much like intimacy, we can have moments of frientimacy with any of our friends at various times—we can also develop relationships that experience it as consistently and meaningfully as we can ever hope to know.

All new relationships start at the bottom of the triangle, where both the actions of consistency and vulnerability are quite low. In this place I will always practice the value of authenticity, but I will be mindful to use the actions of vulnerability only in tandem with the increase of consistency or commitment.

Note there are notches in the consistency and vulnerability arms of the triangle much the way a bookcase has options for different shelf heights. Our goal is to move that shelf farther up the triangle while also keeping it as straight as possible. If our consistency is at a 1, our vulnerability should not be a 4. If we barely know each other, it is not appropriate or healthy for me to expect you to act like my therapist while I process my life in your presence. On the flip side, if our consistency is a 7, then our vulnerability should be somewhere in the 6–8 range. (In the next chapter we'll discuss the various ramifications of not keeping the three elements in equal balance.)

Vulnerability, in its healthiest form, is incremental, thoughtful, and predicated on commitment. It is a two-way street paved by both positivity and the trust we feel from the track record of our consistency.

When I first meet someone, our commitment to consistency is temporary and usually unspoken. If I'm meeting people I'll work with, our commitment is usually something along the lines of "I will do my part to make sure we accomplish our shared goal." Or with a new friend our commitment might flow as "I will show you respect by paying attention to you." Similarly, when parents meet with other parents the commitment would be: "We both want our children safe and happy. I'll do my best for yours and hope for the same from you." We make unacknowledged commitments everywhere we go in life.

Just as important as what those initial commitments include is what they don't include. We are not saying: "You will be the first person I call when I am in a car accident," "I will stay in touch with you for the rest of my life," or "I will call every day this week to check in on you." Those sorts of commitments are reserved for relationships that have traveled higher up the Frientimacy Triangle. Our goal is to recognize how vulnerability, for the most part, is a gift that mirrors the TRUST developed throughout the *consistency* of our commitment.

Let's consider what incremental vulnerability can look like. For example, a woman once innocently asked me, "How long do I have to wait to tell someone that I'm going through a divorce? Is it like the three-date rule?"

Of course, there is a vast difference between what we say to a new friend versus what we'd tell a time-trusted friend. Fortunately, when we're in the process of developing the former into the latter, vulnerability offers us a means of being authentic through an act of disclosure. In the spirit of staying real, it is appropriate to share one is going through a divorce on a first outing with someone—with one caveat. In recognition of the low commitment of the relationship—its little history or non-established consistency—this woman would want the *way* she shares the information to reflect that she doesn't expect her new friend to act like a more-established friend might. In other words, to someone we don't know well we can share our truths authentically as long as we sustain our responsibility, which is to both honor the need for positivity and acknowledge that our commitment is relatively new.

So in this case we might say:

> "I am going through a painful divorce right now . . . and my whole life feels disoriented. But one of the good things that's come from it is my growing awareness that I want to develop better friendships. So I am grateful you were willing to get together, as I look forward to reminding myself that there is plenty of love in this world and lots of fun to be had."

With such an approach we can share honestly while also showcasing that we understand boundaries. The trick is just to remember that the container for pouring out our hearts, hurling our anger, or processing our fears has not yet been developed with the new person. It's not the job of someone who barely knows us to fill in for the friendships we don't currently enjoy. In other words, just because someone opens the door doesn't mean she wants us moving in.

Conversely, if that sample script above was *all* we shared with close friends—those with whom we've developed a high level of commitment—then we wouldn't be practicing the vulnerability that would feed the friendship. We owe a relationship with greater consistency an equal amount of vulnerability.

The value of fostering intimacy is that we can ultimately have relationships that support our every thought—even the ones we cringe to hear ourselves utter. With friends at the top of our triangle, friends with whom we've developed a track record of mutual vulnerability and high commitment, we can share just how ugly the details of our divorce are, how angry we are, how long we cry at night, and how scared we are that we'll never be happy again. We can call late at night, and possibly even stay a night or two on the couch. But that is an honor reserved for only the handful of people who have, over time, developed frientimacy with us.

Embracing Frientimacy

To again consider the definition of *intimacy*, if the people around us consistently exhibit traits of positivity, vulnerability, and consistency, then we'll want to become more and more practiced at saying "I see you" when they share their innermost selves. We'll also want to trust their responses when they do the same. It's our privilege to be more fully seen, and our responsibility to work to more fully see the other.

Returning to the film *Avatar*, Jake and Neytiri say "I see you" to each other at several stages of their relationship—and each time they mean it. Later in their story, betrayal, war, disappointment, and loss lead to Jake having to return to his original, crippled human form. Locking eyes with a man she has never seen and yet still knows, Neytiri whispers, again, "I see you."

"I see you" were the words that scared them the most to say, and yet they were also precisely what they craved to hear. Such is the beauty of intimacy. Within a history of incremental sharing and bonding, when the time comes to reveal ourselves in all our frailty we feel safe to do so—and in so doing can reach a deeper level of connection than we ever thought imaginable.

Worth Remembering

- Frientimacy is any relationship where two people feel really seen in a way that feels satisfying and safe for both of them. To create, foster, and protect our intimacy, we must practice three things: positivity, consistency, and vulnerability.

- For us to feel satisfied, we must feel our interaction is rewarding, practicing positivity with each other. And in order to maintain a healthy balance in each relationship, it's imperative that the positives consistently outnumber the negatives: at a ratio of 5:1.

- For us to feel safe, we must feel some level of trust, practicing consistency with each other. Without a sense of growing commitment, we won't establish the confidence in our friendship that frientimacy requires.

- For us to feel seen, we must be willing to reveal ourselves, practicing being vulnerable with each other. But we must also be strategic and thoughtful, ensuring we reveal, share, risk, and disclose in healthy and appropriate ways.

- Frientimacy is best built with the three requirements—positivity, consistency, and vulnerability—increasing in tandem. And we do that by identifying, and righting, any frientimacy gaps we encounter (which we'll learn about next!).

4

Identifying the 5 Frientimacy Gaps

Most casual relationships remain just that: casual. We don't expect every person we meet to become our best friend, nor should we. But as we deepen some friendships by adding positivity, consistency, and vulnerability, we'll also notice that every relationship is susceptible to one or more gaps in those three areas.

The good news is that we aren't victims in this dance—we can address these gaps. Frientimacy gaps fall into five distinct categories, all of which can be worked through.

Most notable is the fact that identifying a gap can reveal that our discontent doesn't automatically mean our friend is at fault, or not worthy of the relationship. Rather, identifying the gap can indicate that *we* need to add to our relationship, mindfully and heartfully, one of the three frientimacy requirements. As such, our role isn't to regularly dismiss people as their judge; our role is to play friend-maker, regularly adding love—in the form of positivity, consistency, and vulnerability—to the relationships that matter to us. So let's get started!

The Five Frientimacy Gaps

Returning to the image of the friendship being a love bucket: If our relationship is fairly new and starts to leak, we'll want to see if we can set up boundaries to protect the budding relationship from experiencing too much stress too soon, which could doom it to failure before its benefits are fully realized. And note that the deeper the history of the relationship, the more attention we'll want to put to fixing its leaks. I've seen many a relationship crumble simply because a leak was never fixed.

Low-Positivity Imbalance

The first gap is a triangle that lacks a strong foundation of positivity. This lack could fall anywhere on a spectrum from worst to least, with stress and pain at one end and "blah" neutrality at the other end. Note that a mere lack of negativity, while not discouraging per se, nonetheless doesn't encourage us to lean in to a relationship. For most of us to want to pursue something, we first have to feel there's some reward in doing so—and ideally that reward will be, if not joyful, then at least pleasant.

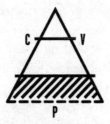

Low Positivity Gap

Since positivity is the FOUNDATION *of frientimacy, we risk leaking intimacy if our positivity:negativity ratio isn't protected.*

Imagine proceeding with a friendship triangle that ranks low in positivity—to build commitment or vulnerability on a platform constructed of guilt, fear, obligation, or exhaustion continually risks the chance of collapse.

It bears repeating: healthy people aren't looking for needy, whining, drama-filled, complaining, negative people with whom to spend time. In the process of working to make friends, our first priority is to add value, making sure we part from any get-together feeling better than we did before. Fostering hope, gratitude, peace, and love is a sweet attraction—one that encourages others to return to for more *and* to offer the same.

If our relationship feels like we aren't experiencing the 5:1 ratio we discussed earlier—meaning we need at least five positive experiences in order to just balance out each negative experience—then we have two options for righting the imbalance: 1) decreasing the negativity, and/or 2) increasing the positivity.

Some negativity, such as a relationship breakup or financial loss, cannot be decreased. Life includes painful moments, so we all will experience crisis and loss. When we see our friends are struggling through rough times, we can strengthen our bonds by reaching out, offering whatever support they might need. Other kinds of negativity—such as how we interpret another's actions, or don't protect our boundaries—*can* be decreased. How? By choosing to show up differently. This could mean working to be less critical, or even just to frown less.

But even if we can't remove all negativity, we can *always* add more positivity. For example, if we're feeling our conversations with a friend dwell too much on something that's not working in her life, we can invite her out to a comedy club and say, "Just for tonight, let's not talk about X. Let's give ourselves a night of laughter." Or we could suggest an adventure—like a mountain hike—that would leave us proud, inspired, and energized. Another approach would be to collect some meaningful sharing questions (there's a list in the Frientimacy workbook for you!) and say: "I thought it would be fun while we had dinner tonight to answer these questions together." Including questions like "What are three things you like about yourself?" and "What do you most appreciate in your friends?" would give you both the chance to express love and affirmation. It's just that sort of love putty that can save a friendship, allowing it the chance to fill up again with love.

Low Consistency/Low Vulnerability Imbalance

Once our base of positivity is stable and growing, we can begin to fill in the gap by incrementally increasing our commitment and our vulnerability, which inevitably will start out low. Why? Relatively new relationships are not fully cultivated—we haven't yet developed our mutual commitment and deep sharing. So it makes sense that they would not be as meaningful as the friendships with a long history of memories and shared revealing.

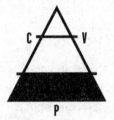

Low Consistency/Low Vulnerability Gap

Most of our relationships have a strong foundation of positivity and small, equal amounts of consistency and vulnerability.

This has nothing to do with how much we may like each other; it simply concerns the fact that friendship is based on how regularly two people repeat the positive actions that build a meaningful relationship. We cannot pinky-promise ourselves to the top of the triangle, simply willing ourselves to where we want to be. What we can do is appreciate what is there—and continually add more.

Most of our relationships will stay in this shape, with a strong foundation of positivity and small, equal amounts of consistency and vulnerability. We simply cannot enter into the highest levels of frientimacy with every person we meet. It exhausts me just thinking about it! Plus, note there is huge value in having relationships with people for reasons other than frientimacy. We feel supported when we have a wide net of casual friends (what I call "contact friends"); we feel like we belong when we have friends in the silos of our lives—at school, at work, at church, in a book club, in a support group (what I call "common friends"); and we feel loved when we have friends far and wide who we know would be there for us no matter how long it's been since we last engaged with them (what I call "confirmed friends").

But if all our relationships are like this, then we won't be receiving the deeper intimacy we crave because we haven't prioritized a few people with whom to intentionally build up our commitment and vulnerability. But once we do identify friends we'd like to build with, we can eventually close the gap by spending more time together and sharing our lives in rewarding ways.

Low Consistency/High Vulnerability Gap

A common gap, one of low consistency and high vulnerability, results when we share too much, too soon, pouring more vulnerability into the relationship than the current commitment level can support. In romance (at one end of the spectrum), this gap often occurs as a one-night stand, or when one partner starts talking about marriage and babies just a few weeks into the relationship (at the other end). And while this high vulnerability might feel good in the moment—to one or even to both people—it's not the path to safe and sustainable intimacy. Our goal isn't just to pretend we're close or feel bonded—it is to actually be close and bonded, which requires enough consistency and commitment to back up, or substantiate, the bonding and the sharing.

Low Consistency Gap

When we increase our vulnerability faster than we develop our consistency, we can exhaust and overwhelm a friendship.

I once worked with a woman to help her assess why she was having a hard time building intimacy. I quickly experienced firsthand that she would basically vomit her life story on people as soon as she met them. She had no problem being vulnerable—hungered for it, actually—and felt frustrated that so many others "stayed too shallow," preferring to talk about subjects that, to her, weren't deep enough. She thought she was helping increase their potential bond by talking about her cancer scare and her rough childhood. When potential friends didn't take the bait, she'd get bored, believing she was too mature for all these people whom she only felt safe staying on the surface—whereas they may have been running in the opposite direction.

Many erroneously believe that the faster they spill their guts the stronger their friendship would be—but it doesn't work that way. Vulnerability without commitment is simply a train wreck with witnesses.

Does it feel constraining sometimes to limit what we share? Of course—as it should. It's only with my closest friends that I should be sharing all the drama, the fears, the processing, and the pity-party of my life. And as I've mentioned before, if I don't have those friends in place, that's not the fault of my newer friends—that's simply the job of a therapist. And it bears repeating that vulnerability is far more than the information we share; it's also the actions we risk in order to deepen the friendship.

For example, consider this text message exchange between two women who were just getting to know each other. In this case, the imbalance arose from requests that sounded more demanding than their history supported, including questions like: "What time do you get off so I can call you?" "What are you doing this weekend? I need someone to do something with." "What kind of music do you like? Maybe we should go to a concert together." Given that the texter tried to force a level of commitment that hadn't yet developed between them, it's no wonder the friendship never got off the ground.

So even though I urge you to practice deepening your vulnerability in a relationship, I also urge caution. So, for those of us anxious to rush intimacy, here are two pieces of advice, adapted from Will Smith's matchmaking advice in the movie *Hitch*:

READ THE SIGNS AND LEAVE THEM WANTING MORE. We *have* to be observant, present, and at peace so we can tell when our energy is welcome versus when it's too soon—the friendship equivalent of kissing a new date too early. We want to leave others excited for the next time with us, looking forward to more—rather than feeling they got more than they wanted.

INVITE, DON'T FORCE. In romantic language, Hitch advised: "The secret to a kiss is that you go 90 percent of the way—and then hold—for as long as it takes for her to come the other 10 percent." Phrased in friendship language, we can do 90 percent of the inviting if we want to get a friendship off the ground; her 10 percent response is accepting our invitation or occasionally initiating on her own. See your energy as a "sampler" gift, by which I mean a hearty but incomplete offering, one that invites the other to complete the engagement. When we initiate, we leave space for the other to meet us.

Ultimately, we want our sharing to match the level of commitment we've established through our consistency. To restore balance, we might need to be mindful about not oversharing while also intentionally initiating more time together so that the consistency can grow.

Our goal is time together; it doesn't really matter who initiates to get us there. If we're the ones who see the need, it might as well be us.

High Consistency/Low Vulnerability Gap

The next gap is the mirror image of the last one. In this case we have a relationship that has withstood the test of some time, but not enough sharing is taking place—sharing that would reflect the trust that has been built.

In romantic terms, this could look like a marriage that has lost its soul: The couple is committed to staying, but they no longer confide in each other or feel intimate with each other. In friendship, this imbalance can present itself in numerous different scenarios, either from the requirements of the relationship not having developed in tandem—so one element grew faster than the other—or from an action that lessens one of the elements, creating a gap. Luckily, the steps to bridge this particular gap are mostly comparable, regardless of the details.

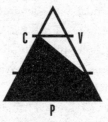

Low Vulnerability Gap

When we build up history through consistency without matching it with shared vulnerability, our lack of disclosure can limit or damage a friendship.

One scenario is in friendships where we've known each other for what feels like forever but our time together isn't frequent enough for us to share our lives in meaningful ways. If we're only chatting on the phone a few times a year, getting together for just an annual weekend, never spending time together alone, or only grabbing dinner long enough to "catch up," then we can feel like the people we love and care about don't really know what's going on inside our hearts and minds. This can be a very lonely realization.

Another common scenario is when one friend finds it difficult to share with too much vulnerability, for any number of reasons. One woman told me, "I don't even know how I feel half the time. How can I even begin to tell someone else?" Another said, "If you had been hurt as many times as I had, then you wouldn't want to share anymore either. I can't trust people. [That trust] always comes back and bites me." And still another woman showed how well she knew herself by saying, "Sometimes I think I'm being honest, but I know I'm still sharing only the things that I really think get me what I want, that make me more relatable, or that somehow is done more for their sake—like, to inspire them or teach something—than it is because I'm taking my mask off and being real."

I have been guilty of causing this gap myself, and I lost a dear, committed friend once because of it. Though I was suffering within the shambles of my first marriage at the time, I chose to not share with my friend just how dire things had gotten. And so she was shocked when we announced our separation and understandably felt betrayed by my lack of disclosure, by my seeming lack of trust in her. I had had what felt like good reasons for withholding the information—partly to protect her from carrying the burden—but the truth remains that I could have taken the risk to reveal my shame. By purposely limiting my vulnerability, I broke our frientimacy. And though this was a long time ago, I'm still haunted by this loss. And in this sort of situation, the gap can be harder to fill—because forgiveness is also called for.

There are many missteps, conscious and unconscious, that can cancel our journey to frientimacy. But whatever the scenario, the truth still stands: We will not feel known and connected in meaningful ways without eventually learning to share as much of ourselves as possible, unfiltered, with people who have proven themselves to be trustworthy.

High Consistency/High Vulnerability Gap

The last imbalance looks good on paper, as substantially more friendship has developed, with only a relatively small gap remaining. But I include this one to honor the fact that even small gaps can leave us feeling something is missing.

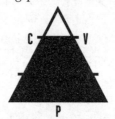

High Consistency/High Vulnerability Gap

Not every friendship is destined to reach the peak. It's perfectly okay to have equal, high amounts of consistency and vulnerability; we won't reach the top with everyone.

This imbalance might exist because a) you're still growing the friendship, and with more time and patience it will invariably reach the pinnacle; b) the friendship has reached a plateau and needs a few intentional steps to take it into expanded territory; c) the relationship experienced a disappointment, and so some trust has been reduced; or d) this friendship hasn't budged despite repeated efforts of growth.

How we'd address the first three scenarios gets covered in the chapters to follow. But to elaborate on the last scenario—when you feel the friendship triangle is as high as it can grow, note that not every friendship is destined to reach the peak. A relationship can only be as healthy as the individuals in it—and we're all works in progress. Additionally, any two friends, however much they might have in common, are still very different people, with different histories and different priorities and different awareness. It isn't realistic to believe that we can reach a peak—a "10"—with everyone. Our goal is to grow every friendship we can, as far as we choose or crave, and then to appreciate what we have with each one.

Besides, to create meaningful community in our lives, we don't need everyone to be a "10." Most of my closest friendships have a small gap of some kind. In one, we don't live close to each other, so we're limited in what we can do for each other. In another, I know she won't consistently open up about her deepest feelings as much as I wish she did, but that doesn't change the fact that our history and vulnerability in certain areas is deeply meaningful. In another, we can talk about some of my favorite subjects—relationships, spirituality, and personal growth—in incredibly deep and fulfilling ways, even though our vastly different lives can seem a bit disorienting at times.

In other words, my life is blessed *because* I have friendships with various degrees of frientimacy. And while any one friendship might have a gap, the fact that I have multiple friendships means that, collectively, my heart needs are still met. This isn't an all-or-nothing game we're playing. When I look at the diversely meaningful group of friends I enjoy, I can see that I don't have an intimacy gap overall. I know with whom I can talk about my marriage, and with whom I most enjoy spiritual discussions. I know which friend to call when I want a fun adventure and which to invite for a quiet party. And I will never box any one friend into only one role, as I want to regularly try to grow friendships into new territory. I also know that if I hit a wall, I can practice contentment for all that we have and share already.

In all our friendships, we are invited to both practice contentment—working to maintain the positivity, commitment, and vulnerability we already share—while also staying open to opportunities to increase the actions that could take us deeper.

Our goal is to grow every friendship we can, as far as we choose or crave, and then to appreciate what we have with each one.

Righting Frientimacy Imbalance

The broadest answer to what limits our intimacy can be answered by asking ourselves, "What is limiting our positivity, consistency, and vulnerability?"

In short, anything that restrains you from engaging in any of the three frientimacy requirements will put a ceiling on your relationships. Therefore, if your schedule leaves you no room to connect with others—making consistency nearly impossible—then that is your answer to what confines you. Or, if you make a habit of whining and nagging and criticizing—obstructing positivity—then that would be valuable information about what keeps your relationships from growing.

To guide you in identifying what limiting behaviors might be at work in your life, I can share with you the patterns I've observed from talking to thousands of women about their relationships. These obstacles, as you can imagine, derive from our three requirements: friends who seem to take more than they give (positivity), friends who don't make the time to spend with their friends (consistency), and friends who think meaningful sharing can result from simply divulging information (vulnerability). All that gets covered in the chapters to follow, so read on!

Worth Remembering

- If frientimacy is a relationship between two people that is positive, consistent, and vulnerable, then it stands that every intimacy gap reflects an imbalance of one or more of those qualities.

- Identifying the imbalance can indicate which of the three imbalances we need to develop in our relationship.

- Since positivity is the foundation of frientimacy, we risk leaking intimacy if our positivity:negativity ratio isn't protected.

- When we increase our vulnerability faster than we develop our consistency, we can exhaust and overwhelm a friendship.

- When we build up history through consistency without matching it with shared vulnerability, our lack of disclosure can limit or damage a friendship.

- Note that not all gaps need to be fixed: We don't need every friend to be a "10" in order to create meaningful community in our lives. Our goal is to grow every friendship we can, as far as we choose or crave, and then to appreciate what we have with each one.

Next up: the foundational element of every friendship—positivity—and where it so often goes wrong.

5

Positivity: Giving and *Receiving*

'm honestly just tired of being the one who does all the giving," she sighed. "I mean, I knew she needed money, so we hired her as a graphic designer for my husband's new company. I'm always the one calling her—we'd probably never talk if I didn't initiate. I helped her unpack all her mother's boxes last spring after she went into a nursing home. And then after that, I jumped into helping her make all the decorations for her son's wedding last summer. It made me realize that I just give, give, give—and get nothing in return. It's not a mutual friendship. I deserve to be in a friendship with women who are willing to give to me, too."

This was one of the rare cases where, as it happened, I got to hear both sides of the story. The "taker" friend in the above scenario noted how the "giver" always called and then just "droned on and on" about her life non-stop for an hour. "I didn't used to mind it so much," she said, "but lately it's just been exhausting. She calls and just complains, repeating herself and her stories over and over. Just because I'm a good listener doesn't mean I don't have thoughts of my own I'd like to share." And about the wedding, "In all the time she helped with wedding stuff, forcing her way into every decision like it was her own wedding, she never once asked me how I felt about my son's upcoming marriage, about my new daughter-in-law, or anything. Never a single question."

There's more. "I'm always listening, spending time with her even though she always picks the restaurants, the movies, and never asks me what I want to do. I can't even remember a time she's ever affirmed me—I'm the one who does that. I think I've put up with her narcissism as long as I can. Is that bad?"

In short, each "giver" felt like she was being taken.

I've surveyed more than one thousand women on this subject. Only 26 percent feel the giving is shared equally, and a whopping 60 percent of us believe we do most of the giving in our relationships. Even the 26 percent who view *their* relationships as mutual tend to believe other women are more likely to be takers than givers.

So we can't talk about giving more positivity to our relationships if we're fearful, tired, or frustrated at the idea of giving anything more. When positivity is low, it's usually not because we can't think of what to add to bring more joy; it's usually because we think we've added our all and it's time for the other person to ante up.

For Reflection: How Do You Rate Yourself on Giving and Taking in Relationships?									
ALWAYS TAKING				PERFECT RECIPROCITY 50/50				ALWAYS GIVING	
1	2	3	4	5	6	7	8	9	10

Obstacles to Our Giving

What has given me pause over the years is how few people feel they're getting more than they're giving. If everyone feels *they* are the overgivers, then where are all these women on the receiving end of all our generosity and sacrifice?

While we will focus primarily on actions we can take to practice positive generosity in our friendships, first let's voice some of the obstacles that create these feelings of imbalance. Which ones resonate as possible truths in your life?

1. Our Unmet Needs

There are more than a few things at play here, not least among them being we're all incredibly busy, tired, and guilt-ridden about how there's always still more to be done. Women especially are justified in feeling they always "do more" in general, whether that concerns housework, childrearing, or being taken seriously in their careers. Mountains of research demonstrates that women often give and do more than their life mates and male coworkers do—all too often not receiving fair compensation in return. So it's completely understandable that we'd not want to approach our friendships as yet another thing demanding our time and attention.

But I believe that much of our frustration stems from a lack in our own lives. When I'm healthy, happy, and whole, it feels good to give, but when my resources feel scarce, my generous spirit can wane, frustrated with anyone who seems to want what I am protecting. Consider the scenario of running late for work: We're likely to get mad at anything and anyone who delays us (we're out of milk, Sally can't find her shoes, there's a long line at Starbucks, the traffic just slowed) when in fact the fault lies with us: for not waking early enough.

We're tired, we have needs, we're discouraged—there's no shame in that. But it's important to realize that the giving battle starts with how much or little we take care of ourselves. We must nurture our own lives before we can feel ready to share with others. The answer to this obstacle is to accept responsibility for taking care of our needs—without expecting someone else to do so for us.

2. Fear of Being Taken Advantage Of

It seems we have a fear that there are hordes of women out there just looking to take everything they can get from us. Or, if not that extreme, that there just aren't enough good women out there who care enough about others to take the time to love them. Regardless, we don't want to be the ones who look weak, who overgive, or who are taken advantage of.

In the book *Give and Take: A Revolutionary Approach to Success,* author Adam Grant claims the fear of being exploited by takers is so pervasive it damages our happiness. He quotes a Cornell economist in suggesting that "by encouraging us to expect the worst in others it brings out the worst in us: dreading the role of the chump, we are often loath to heed our nobler instinct." Even if we're typically happy to give, if we anticipate self-interested behavior from another we might resort to scorekeeping, competing, resenting, or refusing.

But what if that fear is unfounded?

In my survey of over a thousand women, while nearly 15 percent indicated they give less than their friends give them, only 2 percent considered themselves takers. But many of those confessions were tinged with embarrassment—"It seems like a lot of women I've watched give little gifts to each other; I keep thinking I should try to do that but I admit I'm not a very good gift giver"—or were touched with gratitude—"I've gone through a really rough time and my friends have so been there for me. I don't know how I can ever return the favor." These are not exactly the sentiments of crafty leeches.

Statistically speaking, there's no way this fraction of takers receives all the bounty from the rest of us. The far more likely explanation concerns perspective: that in the majority of friendships *both* parties feel they are the overgivers. The answer to this obstacle is to practice extending trust—and to remind ourselves that most women aren't set on taking advantage of us.

3. Responsibility Bias

Psychologists call the tendency to overestimate our contributions as the *responsibility bias*. In one study of marriages, couples were asked to claim responsibility for the percentage of work that they handled in their relationship. So if one spouse answered 60 percent, then technically the other would likely answer 40 percent, since their combined stats couldn't actually exceed 100 percent. But psychologists Michael Ross and Fiore Sicoly found that three out of four couples' sum totals were significantly higher than 100 percent, indicating that at least one of the spouses' estimates was incorrect.

It makes complete sense that we do this, for several reasons. We have more information about what we're doing than about what someone else is doing. We're also more likely to keep track of what we've done than remember what we've seen others do. And we're likely to notice only the giving that matters to us or that is similar to the way we give.

So if in a friendship I tend to be the one who invites my friend for dinner, then my brain might be tempted to think I overgive when I note how rarely I'm invited to dinner in return. But that assessment wouldn't take into account the fact that my friend attends my kids' birthday parties, brings me gifts from her trips, or remembers to call me on the anniversary of my mother's death.

The answer to this obstacle is to increase our awareness of *how* the other person gives and to appreciate each gift. (Later we'll discuss sharing how you'd *prefer* to be given to.)

4. Scorekeeping

In the relationship of the two women at the start of the chapter, one saw herself as the giver because she'd given her friend graphic design work, and yet, the other friend saw that incident as an example of her own giving because she did much more work than she charged for. So the sum total of that exchange exceeded the cap of 100 percent: Each woman awarded herself more "points" than is logically possible for that round.

Scorekeeping is problematic. Do I get the credit for calling all the time, or does she get the credit for listening to me do most of the talking? Do I get points for always hosting girls' night, or does she get points for always driving the distance to reach me? Am I gifting her with an invitation to my special dinner party, or is she gifting me by paying for a night of babysitting in order to come? And talking about babysitting, if I watched her two hyperactive kids tear apart my house all afternoon, are we even if she watches my three obedient angels the next day—or did I give more? Was the generosity in asking my friend a lot of questions about her life, or was the generosity in her being willing to share and reveal all those stories to me?

A problem that comes hand in hand with prioritizing *our* contribution is that we're less likely to thank and affirm the other for her generosity—and more likely to feel offended when she doesn't acknowledge our own. The answer to this obstacle is to challenge ourselves anytime we think we are overgiving: try to see how your giving might be viewed by someone else.

5. Giving Focus: Yours vs. Theirs

It's incredibly easy to assume that people similar to us perceive the world similarly, too. But many who've been in couples therapy could tell you that there can be night-and-day differences in how a "well-matched" couple views the world. This phenomenon can greatly influence how we value different ways of giving and receiving love, and I can assure you that one spouse's gift could be another's snub. It's easy to choose our gifts based on what *we'd* like to receive, but the far more important consideration is what the *recipient* would like to receive.

Without considering the other, we're more likely to throw a surprise party for someone because *we* would like one, plan the fancy tea party for her baby shower because *we're* tired of baby shower games, or buy her a new purse because *we* find her current one shabby. And it's not always because we don't know what our friend would prefer: It turns out that, even when we know clearly what the other wants, we still sometimes choose to give what we want. Research published in the *Journal of Experimental Social Psychology* shared two incongruous findings regarding a wedding registry: When we're gift givers we much prefer to select gifts not on the registry, as we're convinced that's more thoughtful and creative, but when it's *our* registry, we are much happier when everyone buys us the items we actually requested.

The book *The Five Love Languages* suggests that we all tend to feel most loved when the love is given in a form that we value, whether that's with 1) words of affirmation, 2) acts of service, 3) physical touch, 4) quality time, or 5) receiving gifts. If our preferred love language is quality time, then we'd be prone to offering the same to our friends—perhaps being unaware that they prefer receiving gifts, and in fact are still miffed that we forgot their birthdays.

Countless fights in our romantic relationships have stemmed from disappointments around how the other chooses to love us: what gifts they didn't get us, what words they didn't say, what time they didn't prioritize, what actions they didn't do. It would be naive to think we wouldn't feel some of those unmet expectations in our friendships. The answer to this obstacle is twofold. First, we can ask our friends what gifts or actions we can offer that would mean the most to them—and then follow through. Second, we can tell our friends what we'd most appreciate from them.

The Positivity Ratio is 5:1. A meaningful, lasting friendship brings much more joy than sorrow.

Five Practices for Enhancing Positivity

Ideally, every interaction with a friend is an exchange of positivity. We show up, we talk, we laugh, we vent, we listen, we encourage, we validate—we both give and we both get.

When we aren't giving to ourselves or feel drained by life, when we start feeling anxious about the needs of those around us—we're more likely to start engaging in scorekeeping, and then be tempted to give less. But if we withhold our gifts we're not only hurting our friendships—we're hurting ourselves.

Adam Grant's *Give and Take* makes a very compelling case that the most successful and happy people aren't the takers or the matchers (those who tend to keep score or give only when it's to their advantage). The most successful and happy people are, in fact, the givers. The givers have wider networks, more people cheering for their success, more support when needed, and deeper bonds in their relationships. They live with greater trust, and life rises up to meet them.

But giving in to the temptation to give less does more than just hurt ourselves and our friendships—it also hurts our community. Robert Putnam in *Bowling Alone* reminds us that a distrustful society seems correlated to our growing loneliness. I love his definition of "generalized reciprocity": when we offer something to another without expecting anything in return from *that* person—confident instead that *someone else* will return the favor down the road.

I believe we live in a world where we don't need to fear each other. The answer is rarely to give less or to pull away. Rather, the answer for our character development and joy, for our relationships, and for our world is to stay as generous as possible. This also means giving to ourselves so we're not depleted, giving to others in ways that matter to the other and that don't drain us, and giving to friendships by learning how to receive.

To follow are five practices for enhancing the positivity in all your relationships.

This practice concerns *the story we assign to the actions of our friends* when, for some reason or another, we feel they don't care as much as we do.

"I have a pattern of getting into friendships that never feel 50/50," she confided in exasperation.

When I asked her to elaborate she named items on many friendship grocery lists: friends don't make enough time for us, we seem to do all the inviting, they sometimes decline, they don't reach out to offer help. "My entire life I feel like I care more about our friendships than my friends do."

My answer? "That's likely true. And it's okay."

This reply usually inspires protest, with special emphasis on the importance of mutual friendships. But what does "mutual" even mean, really? What we want are relationships where both people are loving and kind, but we have no guarantees of such being shown in the same way or with the same priority and urgency.

We can't expect everyone to be on the same page we are—whether we're setting up a savings account, eating healthily, voting in elections, or focusing on romance. Even those who share these values will rank them differently. Someone who instinctually values safety, comfort, and health will make different decisions from someone who is ingrained to value connection, collaboration, and service—both of which differ from someone pulled toward adventure, stimulation, and risk. Some of our friends will be as focused, aware, and intentional in the development of their friendships as we are, but the chances are greater that most of them won't. But that doesn't mean they love us any less. Plus, we alter our priorities as our situations change, and that's how it should be.

Where this natural variance in priority can be detrimental is if we take someone else's priorities personally, or if we judge others for their preferences. The differences in how others express their love for us doesn't mean they love us any less—it just means they love us differently.

The bigger question is whether we feel the energy we put out brings meaning back to us. In other words, if a friend refuses our every invitation, then that's one thing, but if she says "yes" regularly enough, and we enjoy our time with her, then that's something else entirely. Our ability to soak up what our friends give us is almost entirely dependent upon our perspective.

Friendspiration: "When I give to my friendships, I am giving to myself."

The truth is that when we give to a friendship it is to *our* benefit as much as to our friend. Or, it may be even more to our benefit if we're the ones with the felt need. Whatever we give to a friendship is given right back to us. When you initiate and reach out, you are gifting yourself with time with friends, deep conversations, memories, laughter, and validation. Let go of the belief that you're getting less. Let go of the fear that it means they don't love you. Just spread the love!

FOR REFLECTION: Select one friend and list all the ways you give to her. Now, next to every item note how giving that energy benefited you in some way. For example, the item: "I emailed her to see if she wanted to get together and ended up driving most of the way to her" might include with it, "I received two hours of catching up with her and feeling closer. I also got some time to myself during the drive."

FOR PRACTICE: Work to retrain your brain to go less often down roads of pity and self-doubt; instead, work to recognize more often, and more quickly, that we gain when our friendships are strengthened. How? In between deep breaths, whisper to yourself the following mantra: "*When I give to my friendships, I am giving to myself.*"

This week in particular, do something for a friend, and recite this mantra both before and after you give your gift.

Note that there are two dangerous scenarios where "overgiving" *can* damage friendships:

- *Giving from emptiness*: If the expense of our giving harms us, then we might be giving what we can't afford to give. In the same way that we cannot give what we do not have, we should also not go into energy debt by giving an unsustainable energy loan.

- *Giving for manipulation*: If we're giving in order to feel loved—which amounts to angling for a particular return—then our gifts are neither clean nor pure, and our "generosity" is instead only control or desperation. And that serves no one—especially not ourselves.

Many women give from one of these places and then end up exhausted, hurt, depleted, and mad that their friends "take advantage of them." But the thing is, their overgiving isn't the fault of their friends—even if their friends request it, or enable it. It is *our* job to develop our sense of self-worth so we don't feel we need to give in to feel needed or valuable. And that means keeping our energy reserves in the healthy zone, offering when we can, and saying "no" when we need to.

One of my closest friends and I have a spoken agreement: We promise to ask for what we need, and we swear we will say "no" if we can't. In fact we joked that we both needed to say "no" a few times just to prove that we could trust each other to do so. There is something so gratifying about knowing that, if either of us needs support, it's on *us* to ask for it—not on the other to guess it or psychically infer what we need! And we don't need to worry about imposing or intruding on our friend—it's their job to say "no," not our responsibility to preemptively decide for them.

---

*Friendspiration: "When I give, I want my gift to be
as pure and generous and loving as possible."*

Our friends can help us in so many ways, and I'm not just referring to help like "Can we stay at your place next weekend?" or "Can you help me pack?" Yes, let your friends be those to whom you speak up and ask for direct help. But also let your friends be the ones with whom you practice renegotiating, saying things like, "I'd prefer to not do that, but if you can't find anyone else, let me know and I'll be your emergency backup!" And let your closest friends be those with whom you practice saying "no" and still feel loved. These are all emotional muscles; they just need to be kept in shape.

FOR REFLECTION: If you repeatedly give more than you receive and then feel bitter about it, stop for a moment and consider why you go beyond your limits. What's the underlying fear you're trying to avoid? Or the unmet need you're trying to fill?

FOR PRACTICE: If you have a friend you feel close enough to, or a friend you tend to overgive to, recruit her help! Perhaps say, "I've been realizing lately that I tend to give more than I sometimes can, depleting myself a bit because I have a hard time not jumping in and being helpful when I see a need. It's something I need to work on; would you mind helping me with this?"

Some ways to express how she might help you include:

- "Keep asking me for help, but remind me that I need to practice saying 'no' sometimes";
- "Ask me every day to tell you one thing I intentionally didn't do but could have";
- "Brainstorm with me how I can better fill my own love tank every week."

Practice #3: Admit Your Needs

Sometimes the "fault" in a giving imbalance doesn't derive from our friends but from us. This can happen when we fail to advertise *that* we need, or when we fail to specify *what* we need.

Many personas embody the opposite of being "needy." Perhaps you're Ms. Strong-and-Competent, one of those women who just always seems to have it all together, who prides herself on how much energy she has, what she gives and does for others, and how many of her friends she helps with advice and encouragement. Or maybe you resonate more with Ms. Peacemaker? Or Ms. Fun? Regardless of the details, the intention is the same: We don't want to inconvenience, disappoint, or ruffle feathers. We *know* how busy everyone is, and we hesitate to add to anyone's life by bothering to have needs of our own.

But there are strong downsides to pretending we don't have needs: It denies that we're human, and it robs our friends of the joy of giving. We're not as fun to play with if we only sit at the bottom of the teeter-totter, never giving our friend a chance to push us up. No matter how we got there, there's only one way to right this imbalance, and it's not from our giving less, but from our learning to receive more. I'm inviting you to practice receiving.

Of course, before we can express our needs we have to admit them to ourselves, and that can be a tall order. But at the very least we can confide to a few friends something like, "I'm afraid that somewhere along the line I've prided myself on being the friend whom everyone else comes to for help, so this year I'm going to try to practice being the one who admits to needing help, too. Will you help me? Would you be willing when we're together to make me share something that's stressing me out even if I don't think to bring it up?" In other words, we can recruit our friends to help us get in touch with ourselves—and invite them to be our advocates as we practice our new patterns.

Friendspiration: "All humans have needs; it's the strongest among us that can articulate our own."

Another scenario concerns feeling our needs are unmet because our friends haven't magically divined what it is we actually need. For example, let's suppose that my friend has two units of energy to give me this week. But what if she gives to me by calling—when what I really needed was someone to get me out of the house. In the end she's given her energy while I'm left licking my unmet wound. It's not her fault—she gave to me. It's my fault—because I didn't gift her with my honesty.

It's easy to buy into the myth that help is only sincere if *they* initiate it, but that's really not the case. The point is having our needs met, not needing someone to guess them. And any friend who's willing to hear our needs and meet them is the very definition of sincerity.

FOR REFLECTION: If you ever hesitate to express your needs, consider *why* you do so. Is it because you don't see your needs yourself until it's too late? Or, you do see your needs and feel shame about them? Or, do you not trust your friends to still love you once you expose your needs? See if you can identify at least one reason why you hesitate.

FOR PRACTICE: Pick a friend with whom to practice. Is there a decision you're making that you could share with her? Or are there feelings you're repressing that you could try to articulate? This is such a crucial practice, one that speaks to vulnerability as much as it does to positivity. And I'm not saying go overboard—I'm saying take a small risk. Your friend will benefit as much as you will.

Practice #4: Look for What Your Friends Give

This next one takes a page from Positivity 101: our happiness stems from noticing the good we have rather than what we don't have. Tom Rath in *Vital Friends: The People You Can't Afford to Live Without* says friendships improve our lives "if, and only if, you dedicate your attention to the positive roles people *do* play in your life instead of focusing on what they *don't* bring to your life."

But there's even more to it. Rath's research reveals that 83 percent of us bring different strengths to a friendship than our friend does. Furthermore, none of us brings everything. This just underscores the fact that the goal isn't to have well-rounded friends who are all things for us, but to have a well-rounded *group* of friends—whom and from whom we can benefit in different ways.

Stop and think about that for a second: it's not a flaw in our friends that they don't excel in multiple categories. And while we want our friends to love us, *how* they do that will look different with each. Consider this cartoon: a teacher faces his students—a bird, a monkey, a penguin, an elephant, a goldfish, a seal, and a dog—and announces, "For a fair test, everyone takes the same exam. Climb that tree." Of course, only one of them will pass that test, but we know that those that don't are no less smart, talented, or valuable.

Following from there, Gallup identified eight different roles (see next page) that friends play in each other's lives. These remind us that we all bring with us different value, and that we should allow our friends to be who they are without enforcing expectations on them.

Consider yourself against your friends: do you play the same role for each of them, or are you a "Champion" to some and a "Connector" to others? Now consider your friends against these eight categories: can you identify which role each friend excels in? (Again, we can embody more than one role, but we likely excel at just one or two.) Next, compare your categorized friend list against all eight roles: Are any of the roles being neglected—do you not have a friend who primarily satisfies one or more categories? Your answers to all these questions could provide valuable information to help you know which friends to turn to and when—and what not to expect from all. In other words, greater awareness can ensure that we don't get frustrated with an "energizer" for not sitting and talking about deep topics for hours, nor annoyed with a "navigator" for offering advice.

Friendspiration: "I will look for, and find, the ways
my friends contribute to my life."

The Eight Vital Friend's Roles

BUILDERS are friends who motivate you, invest in your development, and truly want you to succeed—even if it means they have to go out on a limb for you. Builders won't compete with you; they will be cheering for you all the way to the finish line.

CHAMPIONS stand up for you and your beliefs, and they sing your praises. Champions are your strongest supporters, and they thrive on your accomplishments and happiness.

COLLABORATORS are friends with similar interests—the basis for many great friendships. Shared interests are what often make collaborators lifelong friends, and those with whom you're most likely to spend your time.

COMPANIONS are always there for you, whatever the circumstances. You share a bond that is virtually unbreakable. Companions take pride in your relationship, and they will sacrifice for your benefit.

CONNECTORS are the bridge-builders who help you get what you want. These friends get to know you and then instantly work to connect you with others who will share your interests or goals.

ENERGIZERS are your fun friends who always boost your spirits and create more positive moments in your life. They pick you up when you're down and can turn a good day into a great day.

MIND-OPENERS expand your horizons and introduce you to new ideas, opportunities, cultures, and people. They challenge you to think in innovative ways and help you create positive change. Mind-Openers challenge conventional wisdom and allow you to express opinions that you might be uncomfortable articulating to others.

NAVIGATORS are friends who give you advice and keep you headed in the right direction. They are best at hearing your dreams and goals, and then helping you find the path to achieve them.

Adapted from Tom Rath, *Vital Friends: The People You Can't Afford to Live Without* (Gallup Press, 2006). See also www.gallup.com/businessjournal/24883/what -workplace-buddies-worth.aspx, accessed 21 June 2015.

And if the circle of friends you've built up doesn't complete all eight roles, then you've successfully identified a specific gap that you would benefit from filling. (For that, check out my first book: *Friendships Don't Just Happen! The Guide to Creating a Meaningful Circle of Girlfriends*.)

FOR REFLECTION AND FOR PRACTICE: Before hanging out with a friend this week, stop and ask yourself, "What does she most often contribute to our time together?" Then, compare that with your mood and needs. Set your expectations to play to your friend's strengths. (For example, "She's great at giving advice. What specifically could I ask her to weigh in on?" or "She's always so encouraging. Where do I most need that in my life right now?")

Or, think through how to ask her for what you want before she defaults to giving in her area of strength. (For example, "You always give such great advice, but today I actually just need someone to listen and let me vent.")

Practice #5: Say "Thank You" to Restore Balance

Of the various things women wish their friends gave more of, initiation tops the list. I believe this dissatisfaction derives from the meaning we assign to that lack of initiation, such as, "It must mean she doesn't care as much about me as I care about her"—which is really just the nine-year-old in us feeling hurt at recess when no one asks us to play. To test this, I started asking women if their friends' lack of initiative would feel different if the women they invited out expressed gratitude.

In other words, if your friend said to you, "It means so much to me that you invite me out so often. I always love our time together and am so grateful that you reach out. I'm so sorry that I'm not very good at giving that same gift back to you, but I want you to know how very glad I am that you haven't let that stop you from initiating. Thank you!" What would that feel like? Would that shift anything? Would you still feel the same angst around initiating, or would it take away some of the frustration? Would you be happy that your giving has been appreciated?

Almost everyone I asked said it would change the dynamics substantially. Having a friend thank us reminds us—or informs us—that it's not because they don't love us that they aren't reaching out. More likely they are shy, unpracticed, strong in other areas, or wired to think differently. After this clarification, most of the initiators feel excited to know that their giving is appreciated—and are happy to keep doing it.

So, for those of you who struggle with initiating, know that it's possible your friends take that lack of initiative personally. So thank them regularly for the initiative they offer your friendship!

For those of you who are the initiators, it's highly likely your noninitiating friends give you more of something than you give them. Perhaps they feel like you don't open up as much. Or that you don't ask very many questions. Or that you don't often offer to roll up your sleeves and help out. Or that you don't affirm them. Identify what they *are* doing, and express your gratitude!

Friendspiration: "I will regularly thank my friends for the ways they contribute to our friendship."

Even an imbalance in vulnerability can often be restored by acknowledging it with gratitude. I had a friend once say to me, "I always admire how willing you are to share your fears and insecurities with us . . . that is so hard for me. I hope to keep practicing it, but I wanted you to know that even though I don't open up as much as you do, I really appreciate what you share, admire you for it, and am learning a lot from you." That affirmation transformed thoughts like "*Maybe I've said something that offended her*," "*Maybe she doesn't like me*," or "*Maybe she thinks I'm stupid*"—and instead left me feeling closer to her and more comfortable with my sharing.

Affirmation isn't just a gift to our friendships; it's also a gift to ourselves. We will feel happier when we look for—and find—the qualities we appreciate in our friends. In turn, your friends will be likely to spread the love and validate you in return.

FOR REFLECTION: Make a list of your closest friends, noting what they give you that is better, more, or different from what you give them.

FOR PRACTICE: Make a plan for how you will articulate your appreciation to each of these friends. Will you tell them the next time you see them? Will you write them a note? Will you pick up the phone and brighten their day with an unexpected love blurt? Share your love.

Turn into the Skid

Our human tendency when we're hurting, mad, or scared is often the equivalent of slamming our foot on the brakes when we hit ice on the road. But those of you who grew up in a snow climate know that when driving on snow the mantra is "Turn into the skid"—because the impulse to brake can spin the car out of control.

The same logic can be applied to our friendships. When we hit ice, we shouldn't pretend everything's fine and just keep pressing the gas pedal, nor should we panic and brake or swerve in the opposite direction. Instead, it's important to pull our foot off the gas a little—so we can reflect on *why* we're getting triggered, and just what needs aren't getting met. (The "Questions for Reflection" sidebar to follow suggests some questions for contemplation.)

So, let's say you reflected on your dissatisfaction with a friendship, and you take responsibility for addressing it. You'll still want to steer into the skid—by keeping the relationship as full of positivity as possible.

Questions for Reflection When I'm Not Getting What I Want From a Friend

- What am I really mad at? Is it my friend, or something else in my life?
- Am I annoyed that my friend isn't responding exactly as I want her to—am I expecting too much from her? Can I do a better job of asking for what I need? Or going to another friend?
- Is my feeling of overgiving really the accurate picture, or is it possible that my friend gives in more ways than I can see right now?
- If I am overgiving, is it because I'm not receiving enough, or because I'm giving too much?
- If I'm giving too much—why am I doing that?
- If I'm not receiving well (e.g., sharing my needs, being receptive to help)—what could I do to practice receiving more in this relationship?
- What can I ask from her that would help me feel we're righting the balance? Am I willing to do that? How can I do it kindly, without blame?

Remember the positivity ratio? Any relationship that drops below five positive interactions for every negative one is a relationship that will be harder to recover. *If* we can continue to bring moments of joy, conversations touched with laughter, compliments that uplift, events that invoke our adventurous side, and actions of kindness—then we are making sure we have the savings to deal with the harder stuff. There will always be tough conversations, hurtful words, neglect, and unmet needs in a relationship—but none of those means we have to withdraw our goodness.

In an ideal world, when the negativity goes up, so would our positivity. It's the love that will get us through it.

What It Means to Bless

In the religious vernacular we bless all kinds of things: babies, food, marriages, the dying. And many rituals across traditions favor blessing, whether we request one of our parents or send someone off with our own.

Unfortunately, some branches of religions have chosen to withhold their blessings from people they don't agree with—on account of, for example, their sexual orientation, gender, or social/political views. But in so doing, they miss the whole point of a blessing.

A blessing isn't something we *confer* on someone; it's something we *affirm* in someone. A blessing isn't something *we give*, only something that *we acknowledge*. People are already blessed, worthy, and loved. We don't make them that way; we only choose whether we want to see it—and help them see it, too. It's up to us to choose to see the value in others, and to give blessings in life-giving and affirming ways.

May we be the kind of friend who steers into the skid, blessing our friends through all the ups and downs of their lives, and trusting that others will do so for us.

Worth Remembering

- When positivity is low, it's usually because we think we've given more than the other person. So it's crucial to not just "give more"—but to also understand *why* we feel a lack of equanimity.

- It's important to be aware of the obstacles to productive giving: our limited resources, our fear of being used, our perspective on giving vs. taking—even the particular gifts we choose to give.

- We can develop ourselves, our relationships, and our world with generosity: giving to ourselves so we're not depleted, giving to others in ways that matter to the other, and giving to friendships by learning how to receive.

- It is our job to develop our sense of self-worth so we don't give just to feel needed or valuable. And that means keeping our energy reserves in the healthy zone, offering when we can, and saying "no" when we need to.

- Sometimes the "fault" in a giving imbalance doesn't derive from our friends' not giving, but from our not taking. This can happen when we fail to advertise *that* we need, or when we fail to specify *what* we need.

- We will feel happier when we look for—and find—the qualities we appreciate in our friends.

Next up: building trust by strengthening the consistency of our friendships.

6

Consistency: Building Trust

onsider how many times the response you hear to the ever-polite greeting of "How are you?" is "Busy!" Many of us live in a state of time poverty, and use "not enough time" as our reason for not reading to our children (or ourselves), voting in elections, attending church regularly, engaging in meaningful conversations with our spouses, eating home-cooked meals, having more sex, going on vacations, working out, or spending time with friends.

We might even agree that the events listed above matter more to us than the items in our daily schedule, but our wishful sigh that we could engage in our preferred activities demonstrates that we feel powerless to do so.

The belief that we don't have time for meaningful connections is easily the number-one complaint I hear as to why it's so hard to foster substantial relationships. Even with those who feel *they* have time for friends say their friendships suffer because *their friends* don't make time for them.

This is a complex issue, as we live in a decidedly time- and productivity-focused culture. Yes, we are busy, but linked to that reality is also the belief that we *should* be busy. We equate busyness with productivity—which we undoubtedly see as a measurement of our value or contribution to society.

Some speculate that the concept of busyness equaling status derives from our religious DNA in the States, whether from the "good works" of the Catholic tradition; the "Protestant work ethic" of salvation being connected to hard work, frugality, and diligence; or the stereotype of Jewish emphasis on education and wealth. But these days it's not God's favor we seek with our busyness, but more that of consumerism, which readily requests offerings of productivity.

And it's not just work commitments that have increased—so have our expectations as parents, which today can be called at best "focused on quality time" and at worst "helicopter parenting." One woman confessed to me, "I feel like even if I had extra time, I should spend it on a date night with my husband or a one-on-one date with each of my four children. The chance of me feeling caught up enough in those relationships to give time to a friend is hard to imagine."

But we don't even need kids to feel that life is simply too full. One Facebook friend of mine in her early thirties shared:

> *I feel like I spend ten hours a day working, two hours eating, another one or two running errands and doing stuff around the house, which leaves like an hour or two per day to split with my partner and our pets—wait, what about "me time" to recharge? So that means that any time spent "investing in friendships" comes at the expense of sleep . . .*

But just because it *is* that way now, that doesn't mean there isn't another way.

I'm observing a shift in our culture where we seem to be a little more willing to try to escape these handcuffs. While we still seem to value looking busy, we are less likely to want to be busy. Rebel voices in our culture are suggesting that the new wealth is having free time, getting enough sleep,

Can't Buy Me Love: Reports on Happiness Science

In his book *Who's Your City: How the Creative Economy Is Making Where to Live the Most Important Decision of Your Life*, Richard Florida reported that "if you relocate from a city where you regularly see your family and friends to one where you would not, you would need to earn an extra $133,000 just to make up for the lack of happiness you feel from being far from those people."

A study in *Social Science & Medicine* showed that if people volunteered at least once a week the increase in their well-being was the equivalent of increasing an annual salary from $20,000 to $75,000. Another study in *The Journal of Socio-Economics* revealed that having a spouse or friend you see on most days impacts your well-being as much as would making an extra $100,000 a year. And Gallup reported in their book *Wellbeing: The Five Essential Elements* that the 30 percent of us who have a best friend at work are seven times more likely to enjoy our work and perform with higher productivity. Social connections positively impact our health as well: We heal faster from surgeries, catch fewer colds, survive cancer more often, and are more protected from stress if we report having good friends in our lives—all of which contributes to our happiness.

In her book *The Happiness Project: Or, Why I Spent a Year Trying to Sing in the Morning, Clean My Closets, Fight Right, Read Aristotle, and Generally Have More Fun*, Gretchen Rubin wrote, "One conclusion was blatantly clear from my happiness research: everyone from contemporary scientists to ancient philosophers agrees that having strong social bonds is probably the *most* meaningful contributor to happiness."

One such scientist could be Matthew D. Lieberman, who in *Social: Why Our Brains Are Wired to Connect* makes the case that "increasing the social connections in our lives is probably the single easiest way to enhance our well-being" because our modern brains were wired primarily for the purpose of "reaching out to and interacting with others."

In other words, retaining the misguided belief that money is the answer can lead us to pursue two great wrongs: spending a lifetime trying to reach what will *not* bring us peace and joy, all while preventing ourselves from getting what will.

In his op-ed "The Age of Loneliness Is Killing Us," George Monbiot wrote about the devastating cost that comes with the ever-present need to accumulate money:

> *For this, we have ripped the natural world apart, degraded our conditions of life, surrendered our freedoms and prospects of contentment to a compulsive, atomising, joyless hedonism, in which, having consumed all else, we start to prey upon ourselves. For this, we have destroyed the essence of humanity: our connectedness.*

Unfortunately, many of us live in a world that rewards producers: one that gives us pats on the shoulder for working weekends, bonuses for reaching goals, and fame for being rich. It won't be easy to wean ourselves off the addictive cocaine of consumerism—and the dopamine hits we get from receiving money indeed fires our brains just like cocaine does. But we owe it to ourselves to see the truth of where real happiness resides.

and working less. While I don't imagine a siesta revolution, we might prove to be more willing to protect blocks of unplanned time—or to at least make sure we're scheduling in the things we care about the most.

What We *Say* Makes Us Happy, Versus What *Really* Makes Us Happy

The area of my life that has caused me the most angst is definitely my finances. My closest friends would vouch for me on this one—and bless their hearts for listening to the same broken record.

Regardless of the reasons for my worries—working for a nonprofit, choosing freelance work, or drowning in self-employment taxes—the emotion behind the details has been eerily the same: "I just need a little more money!" I soothe myself with the knowledge that I am doing what I believe in and working for causes I know are significant, but let's be honest, my landlord doesn't care about how many blog posts I write, and the grocery store doesn't work on the barter system. Money is what makes the world go 'round—or so we tell ourselves.

And I'm not alone in this angst. The accumulation of wealth—one of our primary life goals—is both the focus of the bulk of our waking hours and the reason for our stress. In repeated surveys the overwhelming majority of us indicate we believe having more money would make us happier. Apparently, we think that having 25 percent more than what we have is what would make us happy. We'd finally feel safe. We'd relax. We'd stop whining.

But even the top 1 percent who own 48 percent of global wealth aren't happy with what they have. A Boston College survey of people with a collective net worth of $78 million found that they, too, were assaulted by anxiety, dissatisfaction, and something we're all coming to know: loneliness.

And yet the science doesn't match up with our perceptions. In fact, numerous studies have shown that increasing our income above subsistence level raises our happiness by only a small amount. What has a stronger impact on our happiness? Our social factors: being married, having friends, the size and quality of our network, our involvement in social organizations, and our participation in societal institutions.

So, what if you believed the myth that money would make you happier? You might be more willing to move away from friends for a job with a higher salary. You might prioritize working late over socializing. You might work so hard all week that you need your weekends to just sleep. You might focus on work rather than on relationship-building. You might say "yes" to a promotion even if it means saying "no" to free time. You might work through lunch instead of meeting up with a colleague. You might believe that performance, productivity, and consumption is what life is about. And you might get to the end of your life and realize that the ladder you were climbing was leaning against the wrong wall the whole time.

Four Practices for Investing in Our Priority of Others

Many of us have heard the metaphor about trying to fit rocks, pebbles, and sand into a mason jar. If we want to fit all three, there is only one order that will work: rocks first, then pebbles to fit between the rocks, and then the sand to seep into the space remaining. Do it in the opposite order and you'll fit in only a small amount of the rocks—because the sand and pebbles will monopolize the jar.

It's possible that right now friendships are a rock that you don't believe will fit into your life—because your jar is full. You're running from one thing to another from morning to night, trying to remember dozens of details at any given moment, living with the belief that you'll never catch up on your ever-expanding to-do list, and feeling guilty that you're not connecting enough with the people under your roof. Your nails are chipped, your house is dirty, your fridge is empty. When are you supposed to make time for friends?

But all that doesn't change the fact that the busier you are the more crucial friendships are in your life—because they buffer you from some of the impact of stress, and they reward you with energy and joy.

Now, I know it will feel scary to take some pebbles and sand out of your jar in order to fit this rock, but if you want intimacy it's your only option. To receive the meaningful benefits that belonging can have in your life, friendship has to be a rock that you schedule the rest of your life around.

To follow are four ways to practice building up this muscle.

Practice #1: Gift Your Relationships with Time

There is no way to develop friendships without time. That's why one-third of the Frientimacy Triangle depends on the consistent time we give each other. Without it, our lives are just a collection of conversations and dinner parties. We can have fun with each other, and share stories—but frientimacy will never develop unless that time spent together gets repeated. Often.

In her book *168 Hours: You Have More Time Than You Think,* Laura Vanderkam showed that most of us actually have the time for what we say we want, but because "we *feel* overworked and under-rested," we tend to "believe stories that confirm this view." But she identified how with each week's 168 hours there is "easily time to sleep 8 hours a night (56 hours per week) and work 50 hours a week, if you desire. That adds up to 106 hours, leaving 62 hours per week for other things."

The problem, she discovered when studying the subject as a journalist, is that we don't decide ahead of time how we really want to spend those remaining 62 hours, so it then gets swallowed up by television, Internet, housework, and errands—all things that "give a slight amount of pleasure or feeling of accomplishment, but do little for our careers, our families, or our personal lives."

Most of those default activities require little energy, either because we do them all the time or because they can get squeezed in without prior planning, but with this default approach we can end up having our lives run by what's right in front of us instead of what's important to us. It takes less energy to browse Facebook than it does to think about calling a friend, but thirty minutes of meaningful conversation probably would have given us more energy and sense of connection than would thirty minutes spent reading status updates. Similarly, meeting a girlfriend for happy hour after work might take a bit more energy on the front-end, but we'll be left with higher oxytocin levels—the "bonding hormone" that's so essential to health it's included on the World Health Organization's List of Essential Medicines—than we would after an evening of watching TV.

In *The 7 Habits of Highly Productive People: Powerful Lessons in Personal Change,* Stephen Covey talked about the difference between spending time with what's urgent versus investing time in what's important. For example, checking email can feel urgent, but few of us would name that task as one of the priorities of our lives. So how do we mend our ways? To simply start prioritizing the hours we do have—to do life differently—will feel uncomfortable, odd, even countercultural. We'll likely initially feel guilt, fear, and anxiety. We will second-guess ourselves, fall off the wagon, and struggle with our changing roles. Why? Studies are now finding that our bodies are so used to adrenaline we can feel *more* anxiety when we *don't* have stress hormones running through our nervous systems. So pushing the reset button won't be easy.

For example, consider the woman with this confession, "I honestly feel I shouldn't do anything fun until the house is clean (I learned that growing up), and since my home is never perfectly clean with eight of us living here, I don't go out very often at all." Rewiring our brains to not listen to our "trained" guilt isn't a job for the faint of heart.

The good news is we know that people's choices are molded over time by our society—and then become self-reinforcing. That means the more leisure time we participate in, the more we enjoy it; the more consuming we do, the more we want it; the more we exercise, the more we love it; the more we sit on the couch, the more we do it; the more time we spend on email, the more email comes in. So we can rest assured that putting healthier patterns of meaningful connection in place will soon be as important as breathing air. As it should be because then our lives would be centered on what we crave the most: giving and feeling loved.

Friendspiration: "I have time for what is important to me."

We have the time—the question is whether we're willing to schedule what we say is important to us. We do ourselves a damaging disservice acting like victims to our calendars, as though they are done *to* us rather than *by* us. In trying to not be my own victim, I've been trying to replace saying "I don't have the time" with the truth "I'm choosing to not spend my time on that"—and let me tell you, that's harder than it sounds.

We can't reach depth with our friends if we only dedicate an hour a month to them. The gift of time is the currency of intimacy.

FOR REFLECTION: List out about how many hours a week (out of 168) and a month (out of about 720) you currently spend on deepening your relationships with friends, including what activities you're doing with whom, and how much of that time is scheduled vs. unscheduled. Now, set that aside for a moment and ask yourself, "If I could structure my life however I wanted, how many hours each week/month would I want to spend deepening my relationships?" Don't worry about being realistic at this point; just note how many hours you *wish* you could dedicate to your friends. What feels right to you? For now, just acknowledge if there's a gap between the time you're investing and the time you wish you were.

FOR PRACTICE: Next week, what is one activity in your calendar that you'd be willing to swap out in order to practice making friendships a higher priority? Reach out right now to someone you'd like to spend time with and offer that time slot!

Practice #2: Be Okay with Inefficiency

With the belief that time is scarce comes the evil stepsister belief that we need to value efficiency above all else.

My first book title, *Friendships Don't Just Happen!*, reminds us that, as much as we want friendships to fall in our laps, they simply don't. You have undoubtedly met people you didn't like immediately who became your friend over time, and you also have met a hundred people you instantly liked who never became anything more than someone you liked meeting. It bears repeating: Friendship is not how much we think we like the people we've met; friendship is how much of a pattern two people have in practicing the positive behaviors of friendship. And that takes time—and relational time in particular is not efficient.

And though we might think our friendships were automatic when we were kids, they were not. What *was* automatic was the consistent time built into our lives that allowed us to cavort with those who happened to share vicinity, age, and schedule. But even then, while we may have picked whom we wanted to be friends with on the first day of school, and maybe even enjoyed them from day one, the actual *friendships* developed over time.

The danger in believing the myth that we can simply *find* our friends is that it focuses our attention on the discovery process *("Are* you *destined to be my friend?" "Are* you?") instead of on the development process. But it's in the development where the real friendship happens. And, ironically, it can happen with almost anyone with whom we decide to *repeatedly* practice the behaviors of friendship.

Our desire for speed and efficiency pressures us with thoughts like *"I don't want to waste my time on someone who isn't best friend material,"* or *"We didn't hit it off right away so she must not be right for me."* As though we only need super close friends—and that we're the best judges of who those people should be.

I won't repeat my whole first book here, but it's chock-full of research about how we're not always the best predictors of who we'll end up bonding with. Indeed, we have the capacity to be far more open to connecting with different people—even those who aren't exactly who we think we're looking for.

One of the most powerful beliefs we can adopt is to trust that no connection is a waste of time. Letting go of the need to categorize every person as either all or nothing reminds us that each encounter can be life-changing, each conversation potentially meaningful, each person some kind of teacher, and each relationship a gift—even if the person doesn't end up in our inner circle. This is in part because a fair amount of what we get from relationships is improved mood—and several studies have shown that it's less about *whom* we're talking with but more about *what* we're talking about that most impacts our mood. It's possible for total strangers sharing personal information to increase each other's "feel good" hormones, boosting their immune systems, elevating their demeanors, and increasing their trust.

We need connection. So maybe we should stop trying to find the perfect friend and pay more attention to simply being present with the friendly people who are already around us. Let's stop letting a friendship agenda dictate our strategic moves and plans for specific people. Instead, let's be open to whom we're meeting and be intentional about spending time with them—and then watch where that leads.

A lunch with a casual friend can be incredibly meaningful—if we are both willing to really be present and share what matters to us. Calling an old friend on the drive home can remind us that we're connected far more than we readily realize consciously. And while enjoying conversation with one nice woman at a party may not feel as "productive" as working the room and meeting everyone, we could nonetheless leave the party feeling much more gratified.

We really don't have to be as picky as we've come to believe we should be. In fact, it's a sign of maturity to schedule time to be with people without needing to judge how the relationship will grow or not. It's the practice of nonattachment, trusting that we can be blessed anytime we have the privilege of sitting with humanity. Only from there can some relationships grow into meaningful friendships.

FOR REFLECTION: Can you identify any relationships where you prioritize efficiency? If so, consider if that prioritizing limits your relationship. Are you willing to trust that there are things to be gained and learned in all our interactions—in ways that can't always be measured or observed?

FOR PRACTICE: Today, pretend you believe that everyone you meet is someone you're meant to connect with. You won't know the reason why, whether it's for their sake, or yours—but imagine that the connection was destined and valuable. Observe how that impacts how you interact today. How do you show up differently? Does it end up taking more time? How does it make you feel?

Practice #3: Initiate Courageously

"But I'm always the one doing the inviting," many a woman has said to me. Usually accompanying the words is a flicker of emotion like hurt, anger, even a sense of betrayal.

NEVER INITIATE				ABOUT 50/50				ALWAYS THE INITIATOR	
1	2	3	4	5	6	7	8	9	10

In my Frientimacy Survey half of us feel we do the majority of initiating in our friendships; and one in four of us feels we do over 80 percent of the initiating. But interestingly, when asked how we rate other women on reaching out, we reported only 5 percent, or one in twenty, do the bulk of the work. Which means we perceive ourselves as doing more heavy lifting than we really are—which, as you may recall, is referred to as *responsibility bias*.

On the other end of the spectrum—40 percent of us candidly confess to underinitiating. We *know* we're not stepping up. But even in this category we think we do it more than others because we say 60 percent of other women aren't reaching out enough either.

Any way you dice the data, only about 8 percent of us feel we're in a 50/50 relationship. That's a lot of women wishing for more interaction.

So what keeps us from initiating more? There are several factors.

- *Temperament*: Some of us have strengths and temperaments that make initiating easier. For example, some of us are comfortable asserting ourselves and planning events, whereas others are not natural organizers and are more likely to withdraw. Note that introverts sometimes need less interaction than do extroverts, so they might initiate less because they crave engagement less.

- *Anxiety*: Perhaps even more telling than the introvert vs. extrovert spectrum is the shy vs. non-shy spectrum. We all have various levels of fears, anxieties, and phobias, and these can play out in different ways. A non-shy introvert (someone who has no problem talking to people but needs to eventually step away in order to recharge) may actually find it easier to plan events and connect with others than would a shy extrovert (someone who feels some initial anxiety about talking to people but is energized once it's happening).

- *Values*: Some people who value their friends may not value them as much as they value their work, lover, or family. Or, maybe they value friendship but have their primary needs met with one or two people, and so aren't prone to seek more. Or, if they were raised in a home where friendship wasn't modeled, then they may simply not carry the same expectation or skillset that others do. In all these cases, it's not that these people wouldn't be thrilled by an invitation to friendship—they simply may not value it enough to look for it.

- *Awareness*: Many people are so busy, using up their energy on so many other things, that they barely realize they don't invest any energy in their friendships. Not surprisingly, the very idea of adding one more thing to a crowded to-do list can be overwhelming.

- *Practice*: The vast majority of people could actually initiate far more than they do, but since they aren't practiced at doing it their "muscles" are weak. With atrophied muscles, it is a lot more work to plan a gathering or send an invitation than it is for someone whose similar skills are well toned and functioning optimally.

In all these cases, let me reiterate that friends' not initiating has far less to do with their desire to spend time with you and far more to do with their skills in commandeering their time and energy. For us to think it's "us" is simply our fear making up a narrative to attach to their behavior—or lack thereof. So there's no reason why *we* shouldn't initiate.

We can mature to the place where we can feel at ease putting invitations out there, assured that a declined offer doesn't diminish our value one bit.

If we value intimacy and consistency in our lives more than scorekeeping, we won't throw our hands up and say, "I'm tired of initiating. I'm done." Nor should we wipe our hands clean and surrender, "Well, I'm just not really an initiator." Rather, your invitation to growth is to build that muscle.

My general rule for someone I want to get to know is I'll throw out many different invitations at various times, starting with something more general like "Would love the chance to get to know you better. When is your typical availability?" I might then occasionally offer more specific invitations, from "I'll be in your neighborhood next Thursday—any chance you have time for a coffee?" to "I'm having a couple of girlfriends over for a game night next month; would you like to join us?" And then I remind myself that any nonresponsiveness on her part says more about her life than her feelings toward me. Instead, I pay attention to what really matters: when she says "yes," when she thanks me for inviting her, and when she seems to enjoy the time we do spend together.

An Initiator Mantra

I am the primary initiator in my relationships—not because there is something wrong with me, but because there is something right with me. I initiate because I value more connection in my life. I initiate because a relationship requires it in order to get any momentum, and I can give that gift. I initiate because this world needs more people who prioritize relationships, and I'm willing to be one of them. I initiate because I'm the one who *knows* the benefit of more connection. I initiate because I am brave, because I value love, and because I am ready for more.

Initiating is undoubtedly an act of vulnerability, which can of course be scary and difficult. In reaching out with an invitation we inevitably feel we're "putting ourselves out there." As we'll see in the next chapter, initiating is not necessarily easier than telling someone about our sordid past. Some fear that to initiate repeatedly will look like we care about them, or our friendship, more than they do about us—which we fear says something weak about us. We can worry that we'll look desperate, or that their saying "no"—again—is a sign of personal rejection. We can feel anxious that we're intruding in their busy lives or concerned that we're being taken advantage of.

Friendspiration: "I can initiate the intimacy I crave."

Extending an invitation to another is as much about getting past our fear of rejection (which we will talk abut in depth in Chapter 10) as it is about priorities or busyness. It is an act of courage.

But despite the apprehension, initiating contact with others is a behavior that's vital to developing meaningful relationships. Someone has to do it, and since we're the ones committed to developing frientimacy we're the ones who need to commit to initiating that time together. The eventual outcome will be well worth the strengthening of this muscle.

FOR REFLECTION: If you're a reluctant initiator, ask yourself a few questions. "What is it about initiating that scares me? Why do I resist it so much? What is the worst-case scenario if I initiate too much? Am I willing to practice initiating more?"

FOR PRACTICE: Whom in your life do you often wish you could spend more time with? Are you willing to initiate making that happen this week? Regardless of the outcome, your muscle for initiating will get stronger. The more you do it, the easier it will feel over time—as you remind yourself that initiating fosters the relationships you want.

Practice #4: Prioritize a Few Friends

"I have plenty of friends but don't feel super close to any of them!" exclaim women of every age. This can happen when we're in our twenties, hanging out in social groups every night of the week; when we're networking for our careers in later decades and feel like we meet a gazillion great people; or when we're in our sixties and realize we've built up a plethora of meaningful connections over the years. Either way, when we get to the point when we realize we want more intimacy in our lives, it's often not from a lack of knowing people, but from a lack of prioritizing a smaller handful of friends with whom to go deeper.

If you were to make a list of your friends, chances are it would include some you feel quite close to as well as many more whom you only see occasionally or haven't known as long. Our goal is to deliberately select a handful of friends from that list with whom we want to develop greater intimacy. Then we prioritize those people.

There's an old saying: "If what you're looking for is water, better to dig one well sixty feet deep than to dig six wells ten feet deep." We don't have to stay in touch with everyone we know every week, every month, or even every year—but we most certainly should know which individuals are important to us to reach out to as often as we can.

Running around the yard digging one-foot holes isn't going to quench anyone's thirst. Reaching water requires commitment to explore one particularly selected area in depth, consistently digging in the same spot. In so doing, we don't give up when there's no water right away; rather, we understand that water is available only at a certain depth—so we keep on digging.

Friendspiration: "I prioritize creating deep relationships with select women."

It's in prioritizing a few women—staying in touch and ensuring we're consistently dedicating time to them—that we move some friends closer to our hearts, into deeper intimacy. And as we continue to grow our friendship closer to the peak of frientimacy, we increasingly feel confident in the pattern and history of our consistent time together.

Accounting for the uniqueness of every relationship, commitment could start looking like some of the following:

- *Communicating commitment*: Taking opportunities to affirm how much our friend means to us with statements like "I always so enjoy my time with you" or "I was just telling my mom the other day how much fun we had last weekend together." Maybe you send texts that communicate "Thinking of you," or send a card that says "Glad you're in my life." Communicate anything that affirms your intention to keep showing up for this friendship. Our goal is to avoid our friend ever wondering how we feel about her.

- *Serving from commitment*: As our commitment to our friends increases, we often will expand our time together from just having fun to also helping each other. We can show our commitment by helping pack up boxes before a move, offering to volunteer for an event she has coming up for work, or proposing that we accompany her on a looming medical appointment. When we cross the line into serving each other we are basically saying, "I have your back. I'm here." We obviously can't do that with everyone we know, but we can with those with whom we are developing deeper friendships. The greater the history and practiced commitment, the greater the acts of service we want to offer.

- *Calendaring commitment*: Growing into frientimacy often includes committing more time for the people we want to prioritize. This can mean decreasing the time in between get-togethers from a monthly calendar date to a weekly date, or it might mean checking in every few days via text or phone, or it might mean planning an overnight getaway with each other. Obviously we can't give this kind of time to all our friends, but as we aim to have a few friends experience frientimacy with us, there is no doubt that time together facilitates the sharing and communicates our significance to each other. We feel supported and known in this world when we feel there are people who prioritize time with us, communicating their commitment to our relationship with their most precious resource.

While these actions would be too much to expect from a new friend, they are what can help us bridge the gap as we increase our commitment in a growing friendship.

FOR REFLECTION: Who are some of the friends you might like to prioritize growing closer to? Has anyone been reaching out to you who you could experiment getting together with more often? What will that mean to you to prioritize her/them?

FOR PRACTICE: What is one action you can take to put more consistency into a relationship you want to prioritize? Some examples might include:

- Ask a close girlfriend if she'd be up for scheduling a regular phone call to help keep the two of you in better touch.

- Every time you're out with someone you want to prioritize, say, "I always enjoy my time with you. Would you be up for scheduling something right now for our next get-together so it's on our calendars?" And try scheduling a little sooner than would be typical.

- Invite all the women you know to join a weekly or biweekly get-together you're starting. This way the women who are willing to make the time will show up more consistently.

- Ask a friend from work if she'd be willing to schedule a weekly lunch together.

Worth Remembering

- It's social factors that have the strongest impact on our happiness: being married, having friends, the size and quality of our network, our involvement in social organizations, and our participation in societal institutions.

- To receive the meaningful benefits that belonging can have in your life, friendship has to be a rock that you schedule the rest of your life around.

- We can't reach depth with our friends if we only dedicate an hour a month to them. The gift of time is the currency of intimacy.

- Letting go of the need to categorize every person as either "all" or "nothing" reminds us that each encounter can be meaningful, and each might lead to more depth.

- The willingness of our friends to initiate is in no way a reflection of us—it's a reflection of them.

- It's in prioritizing a few women—staying in touch and ensuring we're consistently dedicating time to them—that we move some friends toward frientimacy.

Next up: deepening our friendships by mindfully expanding our vulnerability.

7

Vulnerability: Deepening Meaning

We just want you to be vulnerable," said the organizer of a popular women's conference.

Her dream was to pull together hundreds of women to tell each other their personal stories in small groups, inspired first by the women on her stage baring their souls.

In a culture that has long been image conscious and prone to looking perfect, the goal was beautiful: to create a safe place for us to be honest about our lives. But I watched as the attempt at swinging the pendulum toward authenticity ended up, as pendulums often do, swinging too far in the other direction for a few of the presenters, whose soul-baring left them with vulnerability hangovers. Instead of picturing their audience naked, as the trite advice suggests, they felt like they were the ones who'd done a strip tease.

"I've never told that story to anyone before," a beautiful woman said to me an hour after her presentation, a look of panic still in her eyes.

"My mom would die if she knew I told that story," said another, looking torn and slightly guilty.

"I really wanted to admit I had that problem because I know others must struggle with it," confided another. "But now I'm worried about being judged by those who would never do what I did. I guess it's the price we pay—judgment by the masses in order to help a few?" Her words sounded more courageous and convincing than her voice did.

Intoxicated like kittens with catnip, the audience ate it up. Listening to the shameful memories and most difficult life seasons—about rape, anorexia, abortions, affairs, bankruptcy, and divorce—undoubtedly made the attendees feel better about their own lives. To be sure, the process helped the spectators normalize their own painful experiences, warmed them up to disclose more deeply during their own small-group sharing, and helped create a space where women felt more accepted when speaking their shame. But for the speakers who had overshared, my empathy provoked a mama bear desire to protect them from never again confusing the call to vulnerability as simply a parade of their skeletons.

What Vulnerability Isn't

While the vast majority of us won't be tempted into baring all on stage, we face the same dilemma posting our updates on Facebook, making small talk at the office, or sitting at a restaurant with a friend. We reward reality stars who reveal everything on their TV shows, praise bloggers for daily charting their raw journeys, and demand answers to private questions from our celebrities and politicians. We may live in a world preoccupied with the perfect image, but we seem addicted to tearing off the veil every chance we get.

We've covered what healthy vulnerability is in a friendship—any action where we're willing to relax our need to protect ourselves from our insecurities. Now let's consider what vulnerability isn't.

Is a willingness to tell anyone anything the sign of a healthy person? Does being authentic mean we have no secrets? Do we have to tell people the worst about us in order to bond with them? Is sharing our insecurities a strategy to starting a friendship? Is something wrong with us if we feel cautious when we reveal significant parts of ourselves? Does being vulnerable mean digging through our emotional closets?

While we're encouraged to "be more vulnerable," we're rarely taught what that actually looks like, when it's appropriate, and how to practice it safely. That leaves most of us erring on one side or the other: Either we overshare or we bottle up.

If you're not an oversharer yourself, you've certainly listened to one. You've just met her and yet she's telling you her life story. Or she brags about being an "open book" but didn't wait for you to choose to read it. Like adrenaline junkies, oversharers can seem to get more energy the more they expose—all in the hope of bonding with others. And while sometimes it does work, usually the listeners end up feeling more exhausted than connected. The captive audience might open up and share, or even ask questions and act interested—as we all can do when we behold a car wreck—but chances are we'll leave feeling run over. Speeding and weaving between cars might get you to vulnerability-land a wee bit faster, but it comes with far more dangers—and carsick passengers, who'll likely not want to ride with you again.

But consider, too, the one who never opens up. Though she's always polite and kind, we can nonetheless wonder, "*What was she really thinking?*" That's a dangerous question. Given all our insecurities, rather than concluding our friend is hiding something, we're more likely to question if she trusts us, likes us, or would be honest with us, asking ourselves, "*Is she like this with everyone? Is she stuck-up? Is she judging me?*"

In the Frientimacy Survey, I asked women to rank themselves on a scale of 1–10 based on how they reveal and share with others, with a "10" meaning they're an extreme oversharer and a "1" meaning an extreme undersharer. Interestingly, exactly 3.39 percent of women owned each of those two categories. The remainder fell into a standard bell curve, with the highest percentage (18.56 percent) rating themselves a "4"; in other words, we cover the spectrum while leaning just toward undersharing.

For Reflection: How Do You Rate Yourself on Vulnerability?

RARELY SHARE				MUTUALLY SHARE					OVERSHARE
1	2	3	4	5	6	7	8	9	10

Ask those same women to rank their friends? They feel their friends share even less.

But here's the good news: Inviting a dancing skeleton out of our closet is the mirage of vulnerability. Being vulnerable doesn't mean throwing our emotional trash bags in someone else's yard and then wiping our hands in satisfaction of a job well done. Being vulnerable is far more than the stories we tell. The focus of vulnerability is to deepen the friendship, not simply divulge information.

To me one of the scary trends is the popularity of anonymous confessional sites, where we reveal sordid confessions and think we're getting the high of vulnerability. But there's little vulnerability in revealing your mistakes and abuses anonymously and then patting yourself on the back for your honesty—*if* you're not also able to practice that revelation with a real human. We are drawn to these forums because they feel safer, as if we can't be judged. I can see the value of knowing you're not alone when you read what everyone else has posted, but if at the end of the day it doesn't connect us to the people we've hurt and been hurt by, then it wasn't vulnerability—it was just dumping.

I firmly believe vulnerability in healthy friendships should be incremental and mutual, sharing bit by bit. If we don't yet have the foundation of positivity, and the safety of consistency, then trying to clear the distance in one big jump could leave us with whiplash.

Of course, some of us will at times choose to intentionally share more than has been earned—to jump even when there is no bridge, such as on Facebook, in a blog, or to help model honesty in a group—but hopefully we do so from a place of purpose. When we choose to expose ourselves, as the speakers did at the conference, ideally we do so because we hope to inspire or teach—for *their* benefit, not *ours*. This means we've already processed that story with safe people in our lives (not using this audience as our therapy session!) and so can let go of any expectations of safety, validation, or reciprocity.

Many a woman has confided to me, "I'm just not comfortable being vulnerable." All the same, we cannot establish frientimacy without revealing ourselves. Study after study has shown that revealing and sharing is essential to building a relationship and establishing trust. We share because it creates a bond with people we love. We also share because our deepest innate desire is to be accepted and loved—which is predicated on feeling known. To have someone love us, but not know us, feels unsafe.

In a study published by the Society for Personality and Social Psychology, researchers sought a practical methodology for creating closeness between any two people, for which they tested various approaches. What ended up working was just as interesting as what didn't work. Consider the following:

- Some pairs were matched according to shared views or values.
- Some pairs were told the goal was to feel close.
- Some pairs were told they were a good match.
- Some pairs simply engaged in small talk for forty-five minutes.

Which of those would you think increased connection between the participants? The answer: none. That's pretty stupendous information, given how much of our dating or friend-finding includes spending time getting to know each other, believing we're a match, and hoping it will work. But none of those factors leads to intimacy.

What did? "Sustained, escalating, reciprocal, personalistic self-disclosure." In other words, sharing. Some pairs were asked to take turns answering thirty-six questions designed to create a bond between them, such as "What would constitute a 'perfect' day for you?" and "Given the choice of anyone in the world, whom would you want as a dinner guest?"

So the basis of connection is self-disclosure and sharing—as long as it's consistent, mutual, and incremental. These are all elements of the Frientimacy

Triangle: to grow closer we have to reveal ourselves, which is best done when both people share regularly, increasing over time. In short, connecting has more to do with *how* we're sharing than with *whom* we're sharing.

So, whether you're already comfortable with being vulnerable or not, if you seek deeper connection with your friends, you'll need to practice vulnerability with them. The good news is that there are five actions of vulnerability—and while we'll eventually want to be skilled in all five, we can get started with the one we think will make the biggest difference.

Five Practices for Expanding Vulnerability

Each of the following areas of vulnerability is necessary for building healthy friendships. To follow you'll see that we start with our hearts and then radiate outward in four directions, as depicted on the "vulnerability compass." (Though the following acts are numbered for ease of discussion, note that in truth it's best to practice all the acts simultaneously, in increasing waves of expansion, like shock waves of loving vulnerability radiating out from our epicenter hearts.)

Vulnerability Compass

Practice #1: Know Yourself to Share Yourself

While our goal with vulnerability is to ultimately feel comfortable expressing ourselves in a diversity of ways, we would be remiss if we didn't start with our own self-awareness. If we can't hear our own truth and believe that we have the right to express it, then we risk being consistently disappointed that everyone else isn't able to read our minds and give to us in meaningful ways.

One of my friends told me how she recently chose the wrong friend to be vulnerable with because her friend's response to her revelation felt judgmental. I asked my friend to describe what response would have felt better; ultimately she didn't know. Yet she was hurt that her friend didn't know either! All too often we go through life only knowing what we don't want. But much more beneficial would be identifying ahead of time what we'll need in any given moment. It's not everyone else's fault that they don't know what we're feeling; it's our responsibility to tell them.

Self-Awareness

The first step in increasing vulnerability is through self-awareness:
knowing our hearts, and believing we're worth being known.

And to tell *them* we have to first do two things: believe that we are worth being known, and be willing to know ourselves. Self-worth is built on self-awareness—the commitment to know who we are and who we aren't, and to believe in our unique potential. Self-awareness is a prerequisite to self-respect because we can't honor that which we don't know or value. And if we can't figure out who we are, and why that matters, then how can we expect others to?

Self-awareness and self-worth are so foundational to healthy relationships it gets its own chapter in part 3 (chapter 9), but I include it here as well because it's also the core of vulnerability. If vulnerability is the risk of letting others see us, we have to first know who that "us" is.

Friendspiration: "It's my responsibility to know what
I'm feeling—and then to share that with others."

How can we practice this form of vulnerability? We might say to a friend "I so appreciate your advice, but what I really need right now is for you to just listen and tell me I'm not crazy for feeling this way." Or, we might share in our safer relationships something like "Right now I'm falling apart, so I would really love for you to come be with me. I know it's a big ask as your life is full and busy, too, but if there's any way you can be here, it would mean a lot." The gift in this is learning to hear our own wisdom whisper what we need and what would be meaningful—and then developing friendships where we don't have to be mind readers, but can come to trust each other to tell us how we can best love each other.

FOR REFLECTION: On a scale of 1–10, how do you rank yourself on being able to accurately name your feelings and needs? How about on being able to share them with others?

FOR PRACTICE: Based upon the answer to your reflection—what is one thing you could do to take a small step forward in either paying more attention to your feelings or in sharing them with others? When can you practice that?

Practice #2: Initiate New Activities

"When I'm with my friends," my client shared, "our conversations are honest and real, so I don't know what more I can do to increase the vulnerability in our relationship. I tell them everything."

Two years earlier she had met a group of friends through my website GirlFriendCircles who got together for dinner once a month. She felt close to them and loved the time they spent together. But she didn't feel they were getting to the deepest level of friendship—and wanted to know if there was something more she could do.

Probing further, we uncovered she felt comfortable and connected with them but also wished for someone to talk with after work sometimes—someone perhaps available for a spontaneous shopping trip or who'd be up for pizza and a movie on her couch.

"How do you know the others don't want those things?"

She shrugged and said, "All our events are planned several weeks out via email."

"Couldn't you just text them this weekend and see if anyone is up for doing something?"

But I already knew what her answer would be. Their friendship, like many, had developed a rhythm of what's "normal." Anytime we go above and beyond that, we walk into new territory, and anytime we're in foreign land, it's inevitable we'll feel vulnerable.

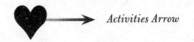 *Activities Arrow*

The first way we can expand the vulnerability compass is by engaging in new activities outside what we've established as "normal."

We can feel nervous about intruding in others' lives, scared we want something they don't; this can then trigger feelings of rejection, and fears that we're too needy. Offering some vulnerability might feel awkward, might create anxiety, might cause us to worry what others will think of us. It's like choosing to color outside the lines when we've been taught to stay within certain boundaries, or breaking out a few new dance moves even though they aren't in the routine.

All relationships, even new ones, develop a dance. The learned dance steps for each individual relationship determine what's "normal" in how often we talk, what methods of communication we use, how often we get together, and what we do when we share time. Whether our time together is usually spent one-on-one, as couples, as families, or in a group of mutual friends, the habit creates an expectation. That habit then deepens around the activity our shared time centers on, be that a job, a book club, or morning walks. Each of our friendships is shaped by whatever actions we've repeated within them.

Friendspiration: "I am gifting myself with fun when I invite friends into new activities."

Some might say every relationship *falls* into a rhythm, but that suggests we're victims of circumstance. And just the opposite is true. *We're* the ones who codeveloped that rhythm—having helped decide the tradition of every friendship in our lives. So it's up to us to invite the friendship into a deeper and more meaningful place. We do that both by expanding the territory our friendship covers and by broadening the way we interact with each other. Time together is what elongates our bridge. Every time we're together we add a slat to the bridge—which ultimately leads to the bonding we long for.

FOR REFLECTION: Ask yourself, "What holds me back from initiating more consistent or expanding activities with the friends who are important to me? How might I think about this obstacle differently to move me in the direction of intimacy?"

FOR PRACTICE: Pick one friendship to experiment with by adding a new activity. Who will you invite, what activity might you do, and when should you do it?

Ideas for New Activities

DARING: Invite a friend from one container of your life (e.g., work, church, kids' school) to do something completely outside that one shared area.

AMBITIOUS: Think of two to three really fun things you want to do this year that might take planning ahead of time. (Camping? Attending a musical? Girls' weekend in the city?) Commit to finding friends to join you.

EXPERIMENTAL: Try to think of one memorable activity to shake things up a bit with a close friend. Can't think of one? Well, what might you want to take a picture doing? (Hot air balloon? Wine-tasting? Piloting a tandem bicycle?)

IMPROMPTU: Commit to once or twice this month reaching out to someone with a last-minute invite. For example, "I'll be in your neighborhood tonight—any chance you can meet up for a drink?" Or, "Hey, if I were to show up with Chinese takeout tonight, would you be up for watching TV together?"

ROUTINE: Sometimes the best thing we can do is invite someone to do the things with us that seem small—perhaps grocery shopping together, getting manicures, meeting at the Farmers' market, or walking around your neighborhood.

One of my dear friends once called me and said, "I want to follow up on the conversation we had last week to see if I hurt your feelings when I was processing *my* feelings about extroverts."

Being an extrovert, I know that sometimes my energy can be a bit like a wave pounding the shore. I had walked into her house with gusto to spare, hugging her kids, laughing, and asking lots of questions. She described my energy as being so high that she felt little of her energy was needed—leaving her feeling she was low energy in contrast.

I won't lie, even though I knew she was just trying to share how it felt to be in her shoes, it did sting a bit to hear that. My instincts were to pull up the drawbridge and go into protection mode.

"*Do I exhaust people?*" I had wondered. And was it my job to turn down my volume when I walked into a room? Questions and fears arose, but I begged myself to not take it personally and to keep the focus on what she was trying to share about *herself*.

We had kept the conversation going at the time, both of us exploring our personalities, trying to be sensitive, and yet undoubtedly stepping on each other's toes a bit. We ended that night apologizing if we had said anything that hurt the other, and we certainly both knew to our core that we were loved. Indeed, we had both skated on thin ice with a few of our comments—which is exactly what can happen when two people show up with transparency and vulnerability. Fortunately, our history and commitment was strongly developed, and we had practiced many uncomfortable conversations before.

She could have chosen to move on, breathing a sigh of relief that we'd made it through that conversation. Instead, she chose to bring it up on the phone the following week, which gave us a chance to revisit the process. In doing so, she offered us the gift of taking our relationship deeper.

Conversation Arrow

*A second way we can expand the vulnerability compass
is by adding new topics of conversation.*

Talking *about* our relationships is as important as having relationships. It's one thing to go to an event together; it's quite another to debrief afterward. ("What was your favorite part? How did it make you feel?") Similarly, it's one thing to have a hard conversation; it's quite another to talk about how we did, what we felt, and what we can learn from it.

As for my friend and me, we ended up affirming each other for how safe it feels to be in our relationship. We know we'll disappoint each other, be jealous of each other, and potentially judge one another—all while knowing we can always talk about it and always trust each other. And our relationship deepened in big ways through those conversations. Did it feel vulnerable? You better believe it! Everything about it did, from sharing how it felt to have our individual personalities to then sharing how we felt misunderstood or defensive afterward.

But we can expand conversation even when we don't sense tension or misunderstanding. For example, in the study involving the thirty-six sharing questions, about a fifth are about the relationship in general. Questions such as "What do you like best about our friendship?" and "Is there anything you've ever wished we could do together that we haven't yet?" remind us that there is an *us*—not just a you and a me.

We can also expand communication by sharing what we need from each other, discussing new subjects, learning how to ask questions and listen well, being curious about each other's pasts, and sometimes engaging in expansive topics far bigger than our circumstances and updates, like politics, spirituality, dreams, or ideas.

Anytime we're willing to take our conversations off the beaten path, we expand the territory of that friendship. As we practice talking about different subjects, we take topics off the taboo list (or at least off the "never been there" list)—and instead feel more confidence in the friendship, knowing there are few subjects we can't discuss. As we successfully share deeper and wider subjects, we build trust in our relationship—so, instead of being friends who mostly update and chat, now we've practiced being girlfriends who know we can also talk about sex, feminism, and the latest book we read.

After a get-together, ask yourself:

"What percentage of the airspace did I take up this evening? Was it in ratio with the number of people connecting? Whatever fraction I made up of those in the room—one of two? one of five?—did I talk for only that same fraction of the time? Did everyone else feel I gave them their equal share?"

If you realize you "took up" more time than your share, consider how you might become more mindful of this tendency in the future.

Another way we can expand our vulnerability through communication is in shifting the quantity of our talking to better match that of our friends. So that would mean talking less if we are used to talking a lot, or talking more if we're used to being the quiet one. Choosing to practice showing up, especially when it's easier to just listen, is a conscious choice that gifts our friendships, and the reverse is just as true. Another way to build trust is in learning how to be okay with quiet pauses in a conversation. Just because we can talk all night, it doesn't mean we should. For a talker, one way to offer vulnerability would be to practice reserve. And while it might feel weird, even scary, to have conversation pauses, trust that new things can emerge in the space currently carrying your monologue.

To recap, the first arrow of vulnerability is to expand activities so our time together can *lengthen* our bridge. In practicing more ways of communicating, we start to *widen* that bridge so there is room to walk beside each other, room to get lost in conversation—even room to step on each other's toes at times. We want the opposite of a tightrope. We want width, which tells us we're not just getting somewhere—we're also enjoying the journey along the way.

FOR REFLECTION: Of the five ideas for expanding conversations in the Ideas for Expanding Conversation sidebar (to follow), which one is least present in your relationships? Do any of them scare you? Why do you think that is?

FOR PRACTICE: Do you think you'd be willing to intentionally practice one of the ideas for expanding conversations in one of your relationships? If so, ask yourself: with whom, how, and when?

Ideas for Expanding Conversation

SUBJECTS: Introduce new topics to the friendship: body image, say, or why your faith is important to you. Express curiosity: Ask what it was like growing up, or what she both enjoys and finds stressful about being a parent.

MOODS: If your time together often focuses on complaining or venting, ask her what she's enjoying in her life these days. If the time together is always polite and cheerful, consider sharing an area that's causing stress in your life.

NEEDS: Practice asking for what you need when you're sharing a story: Tell her whether you're seeking brainstorming, advice, empathy, questions, or encouragement. And when your friend shares a story, ask how you can best be helpful to her without jumping to your default response style.

FOLLOW-UP: Sometimes the best way to deepen a friendship is to ask follow-up questions. Express curiosity when she's sharing and call her after a big event and ask how she felt about it. Even more important, demonstrate the courage to follow up after anything that was uncomfortable; checking in with a willingness to talk more about awkward sessions is relationship gold.

STYLES: One of the best gifts we can give our relationships is the commitment to learn and practice new communication skills: sharing our feelings, making nonblaming statements, negotiating, and saying "no."

"I cannot wait until you're walking down the red carpet," said one of my girl-friends, her enthusiasm and sincerity clearly visible in her eyes. Incredulously—I'm not what anyone would confuse with glamorous, and I had no ambitions in Hollywood—I asked what she was talking about. "You shine wherever you go," she replied. "Mark my words . . . you'll walk a red carpet someday."

I laughed. The only red carpet in my life was the hand-me-down rug collecting lint in my office. At the time I was rebuilding my life, starting a new career, barely able to pay rent every month, and unable to land even gratis speaking engagements.

But while I laughed and dismissed her words, I cherished her intentions. And that day she planted a seed in our friendship: Here was a woman promising to be happy in my success, someone who believes in me more than I believe in myself. And her cheerleading was contagious; without realizing it, I silently vowed to be the same friend to her.

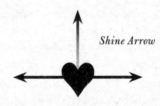

Shine Arrow

A third way we can expand the vulnerability compass is by proudly shining in front of our friends—while also generously affirming them.

How many of us can say that our friends would be thrilled for our getting pregnant, being recruited for a job, selling our artwork, turning heads with our beauty, or buying our dream house? On the contrary, I find that many women feel jealousy and judgments are decaying their friendships—if not outright destroying them. (I devote two entire chapters in part 3 to this subject.) Furthermore, a recent trend among women suggests we're more comfortable sharing our complaints and frustrations (usually about others rather than about ourselves) than we are sharing our accomplishments and joys.

A long-distance girlfriend, confiding to me that she was redoubling her efforts to lose weight, expressed regret that she feels she's always talking about her body image woes with me but never gets to celebrate the results with me. The last time she hit her goal she ended up getting pregnant before I saw her. Two years later, she still wishes I could have seen her at her target weight. She said, "You're the one who has to listen to me whine; you should have been the one to see me at my most proud!" We see each other only about once a year, but because I know how important it is to shine in front of each other, we vowed that next time she reaches her goal we will plan a weekend together and take lots of photos. Celebrating our happiness is fundamental.

One of the most undervalued acts of vulnerability is supporting each other's success in this world. It takes incredible courage to tell our friends they are right, they are loved, they are seen, they are good, they are safe, and they are strong. It takes courage because it can be scary to shine a spotlight on others if we feel something lacking in our own lives—especially since we need to believe those very things about ourselves, that we are loved, seen, good, safe, and strong. It takes courage to be willing to show up fully in front of our friends, and to be willing to receive their love, too.

Friendspiration: "I am a bright light in this world—as are my friends."

I've had friends confide that they feel guilty about making good money or making significant purchases if their friends are less financially endowed. I've heard women say that they underplay how great their family vacation was so that their friends don't feel jealous—jealous because they can't afford a trip, can't get time off work, or don't have a family. I know I've been guilty of not talking about how good my marriage is when I sense others aren't as happy in theirs. Yes, we want to be sensitive to others' feelings, but there's more to it than that: We also want to fit in. We want to be liked. We want to be relatable. We sense we are judged for our positive traits as much as we are for our negative ones. We can be so fearful of being seen as arrogant, or so desperate to want to fit in, that we can unnecessarily minimize ourselves or dim our lights. Humility, though, isn't thinking less of ourselves—rather, it's *not* thinking less of others.

Ideas for Shining

CHERISH YOUR LIFE: While we want to be honest about the fact that some areas of life aren't ideal, we also want to actively identify the areas that *are* good—and be honest about them. Practice saying, "I'm really fortunate that I don't struggle with X, but I'm sensitive to those who do. And while I certainly struggle in other life areas, in this one I want to appreciate what I do have."

AFFIRM HER LIFE: Whenever you think of it, affirm everything you can think of about your friend. The number one value of friendship is to boost positivity by communicating acceptance—so cheer for her parenting style, her work ambitions, her beauty, her big heart. Everything.

INVITE HER BRAGGING: We need to practice owning our strengths and joys, but we're all scared to do it, afraid people will think we're arrogant. So help encourage it in her by asking her questions that invite her to share what she's proud of. ("When do you feel most powerful at work?" "What makes you feel the most beautiful?") Encourage her to really feel her successes!

INVOKE HER GRATITUDE: Women are known for brushing off compliments or dismissing praise. So, when our friend deflects affirmation, we can gift our friendship with positivity by playfully making her say "thank you" or by saying, "Wait, that was a huge thing you just accomplished; are you taking it in and really feeling it? Because you deserve it!"

REVEAL YOUR ACCOMPLISHMENTS: Our friends should be those with whom we feel the safest celebrating our successes, so we need to practice sharing those successes—without being asked. Text her, "Just wanted to share: X just happened!" Or tell her, "I'm feeling more scared than excited that I just bought a house. Any chance you're free to help me step into celebration mode? Takeout at my place?"

If we're going to go deep with our friends, sharing our stresses with each other, then we also need to go high, sharing our successes. We'll talk in more depth about shining, despite the risk of jealousy, in chapter 13. Healthy relationships bear witness to our power, our happiness, our joys, and our talents. So we'll want to build strong muscles that give us permission to be happy and strong—and help us to practice the same with our friends.

FOR REFLECTION: Which do you find more difficult: to receive the affirmation of others, or to give it? Do you know why that may be?

FOR PRACTICE: Pick a friend you believe in—and share with her how much you admire her by describing specific, inspiring things you see her do.

Practice #5: Share Shame and Insecurity

A really good friendship is one where we eventually feel just as comfortable sharing our good news as our bad news—knowing that we're loved deeply regardless.

Shame Arrow

The fourth way we can expand the vulnerability compass is by sharing our insecurities. In doing so we anchor our relationship.

I love to ask my friends the following, "What's one thing you're celebrating or enjoying these days?" and "What is one thing causing you stress right now?" These two questions are like dice, contact lenses, chopsticks, or socks—you never want just one of them.

Sharing our insecurities and shame is the action we most often associate with vulnerability, and it's definitely an important one. Like anchors, when we practice sharing the hard things, we end up grounding and rooting our friendship in the most important aspects of our lives.

This sharing could include revealing events from our past, actions we regret, and moments that made us feel unlovable or unworthy. But far more significant than what happened back then is practicing sharing where we feel insecure or worry *now*.

At my Tuesday night girls' group we always share both our highlights and lowlights—so as to ensure that nothing weighing on our hearts is left unheard. That means that, while my close girlfriends will toast the publication of this book, they also had a front row seat to the lesser-broadcasted feelings, those less obviously felt during a seeming success. They'll remember how I felt too busy one summer to write a book proposal, my months-long difficulties in articulating exactly what I felt compelled to say, how insecure I felt when publishers turned me down, and how much pressure I put on myself trying to write the book I felt in my heart. It will be so meaningful to celebrate this book coming out with women who intimately know that a success is no small thing—that it is by no means all flowers and party hats.

Friendspiration: "My insecurities are beautiful and very much a part of who I am."

And the mutual sharing of insecurities, stresses, and shame means that I have the sacred privilege of hearing about the grief of miscarriages, the agonizing wait for a kidney transplant, the emotional roller coaster of marriage to someone who suffers from depression, the angst of losing a mother, and the pain of being ostracized from a religious community. What a gift that is: to be able to empathize with other humans doing their best in a world that can sometimes hurt—without having to go through every pain firsthand. In fact, that's the very reason humans are attracted to story: to learn (and experience in our imaginations) how others have survived their life journeys. What a gift it is to regularly witness—as each of us figures out what to do, where to live, and who to live with—the beautiful unfolding of the lives of those we love.

There is great healing in sharing within safe relationships. Speaking our shame brings light into the darkness and disproves the voice that says those things make us less than. The gift is being reminded that we are worthy even when we feel shame.

Ideas for Sharing Insecurities

COMMUNICATE ACCEPTANCE: Our friends' greatest fear when sharing their insecurities is that they'll be judged or rejected. So when a friend dares to share with you, always quash that fear immediately by validating, empathizing, and appreciating—and praising her for her courage in sharing.

ACKNOWLEDGE DUALISM: Few events in life are all good or all bad; most are a combination of the two. So, when appropriate, reveal the costs as well as the gains, the endings and the beginnings, and the challenges as well as the successes. Anything else is only half the picture!

INVITE HONESTY: Most of us are willing to share, but we like to be asked, so choose to be the friend who checks in with others. Asking "How are you feeling about your son starting kindergarten?" or "How are you holding up during this job search?" tells them it's okay for them to share their journey with you—and that you genuinely care about them.

SUFFER WITH OTHERS: Practice reaching out to someone when you're hurting. Don't wait until you see each other a while from now: Give yourself the gift of being seen *now*, and model that it's okay for your friends to do the same. Friends want the chance to help and support—don't rob them of an opportunity to be there for you in your time of need.

FOR REFLECTION: What is the hardest part of sharing your insecurities? Do you fear looking weak, being rejected, or appearing needy? What story do you tell yourself that might prevent you from revealing your needs?

FOR PRACTICE: What area of your life right now feels the most stressful to you? Are you willing to commit to talking about that with someone—someone whom you haven't yet told but whom you feel you could trust?

How All Five Practices Work Together

The areas of vulnerability have been broken down so as to encompass distinct behaviors. But, as they are all connected, they need to be done in tandem. Our goal isn't just to practice one act—heading in just one direction—and drive until we hit a brick wall. We don't want a relationship that practices new activities for years without also matching it with expanding communication, nor do we want a relationship that focuses on only the positive without also acknowledging the negative.

Vulnerability Compass

Starting from the center, we'll want to expand our relationships simultaneously into all four directions of vulnerability.

So, starting from the center—represented by a heart that reminds us that all sharing stems from a place of self-worth (practice #1)—we can deepen our intimacy with friends in mutual, incremental, and consistent ways. We do this by mindfully working to grow our relationships with the remaining four practices: *simultaneously* initiating new activities, expanding conversations, shining in front of each other, and sharing shame and insecurity. (See "Tracking Courage Growth: The Vulnerability Compass" in the Conclusion chapter to see how to measure that growth.)

Think, too, in terms of expanding the territory of our friendship. I want my circle of *how* I love my friends to continually expand, so I continually work from my heart outward.

As scary as vulnerability can feel, being willing to take emotional risks is necessary for developing intimacy. Why necessary? Because a sense of truly belonging can only emerge when people show up authentically.

My craving for being liked often pushes me to put my best self forward. In an age where marketers tell us that we are all a brand, the temptation can be to carefully present only that which reflects whom we want to be or whom we want others to see. The downside to that approach is that we can be left wondering if those who claim to like us really know us. To feel authentically loved, we have to feel authentically seen—even if it feels scary. If we want friends to love *us* and not our image, we need to let them see us.

Unfortunately, I think much of society encourages everyone to look the part of the loyal (read: obedient) woman or the upstanding man, preferring to forget that in each of us is a messy, imperfect, scared, and often lonely person. Similarly, the world does the same to us—telling us what we need to look like and act like in order to be acceptable, to be impressive.

We are all at risk of showing only our best sides, extending invitations only when it feels completely safe, discussing only subjects that don't make us squirm, and engaging in only the activities that feel familiar and known. But intimacy invites us to go beyond the façade: to stand and sing karaoke because we value laughter and bonding more than impressing, to ask for what we need because we value depth as well as comfort, to explore a full range of feelings because we value honesty more than we do platitudes, to extend a second invitation because we value consistency more than we do scorekeeping, and to practice sharing what's good in our lives because we value life-affirming connections more than we do hiding our light so as to pretend to blend in.

Vulnerability is a call to stretch the edges, to widen the circle, to be seen, and to see. And yes, one can choose to do that from a stage in order to impress the audience or teach from experience. But far more crucial is when we reveal our vulnerabilities in order to relate, to connect, and to build bonds with others committed to increasing intimacy with us.

Worth Remembering

- In a friendship, healthy vulnerability is any action where we're willing to relax our need to protect ourselves from our insecurities.
- If vulnerability is the risk of letting others see us, we have to first know who that "us" is.
- Every relationship develops a pattern of what's normal, so it will feel vulnerable to initiate new or more frequent activities or bring up previously undiscussed topics. But these acts of vulnerability are crucial to expanding the territory your friendship covers and broadening the way you interact with each other.
- Talking *about* our relationships is as important as having relationships. One of the best gifts we can give our relationships is the commitment to learn and practice new communication skills.
- One of the most undervalued acts of vulnerability is supporting each other's success in this world.
- Like anchors, when we practice sharing the hard things, we end up grounding and rooting our friendship in the most important aspects of our lives.
- We can deepen our intimacy with friends in mutual, incremental, and consistent ways by *simultaneously* engaging in new activities, expanding our communication, shining in front of each other, and sharing shame and insecurity.

Next up: addressing the primary obstacles that can stand in the way of frientimacy.

PART 3

Obstacles to Intimacy

Now that we've discussed the three ingredients that build frientimacy (positivity, consistency, and vulnerability), we'll want to demystify some of the thoughts that can block us from reaching the peak.

Fear is an interesting dynamic. At times it saves us: It keeps us from rushing out into the street and getting hit by oncoming traffic; it keeps us from trusting dangerous people who intend to hurt us; it can even just keep us from making fools of ourselves.

But fear can also paralyze us: It can hold us back from stepping into the very experiences that would expand and deepen us—or even encourage us to walk away from what we want. And it can short-circuit our learning and growing.

There are two things about fear that are particularly pertinent to our discussion: 1) It doesn't distinguish whether it's based on reality or not; and 2) Many of the fears that plague us all are frequently injurious to relationships. So in the upcoming chapters we're going to evaluate five fears that often paralyze us from pursuing the frientimacy we long for:

- Chapter 9: Doubting Our Self-Worth—or, really, the fear that *we're* not good enough.

- Chapter 10: The Fear of Rejection—or, really, the fear that *they* don't think we're good enough.

- Chapter 11: The Toxic Friend Trend—or, really, the fear that *they* aren't good enough.

- Chapter 12: Jealousy and Envy—or, really, the fear that *they're* too good.

- Chapter 13: Holding Ourselves Back—or, really, the fear that they think *we're* too good.

But first: Chapter 8—where we'll consider the benefits of Leaning In to Intimacy, even when doing so feels scary, difficult, or awkward. Onward!

8

Leaning In to Intimacy

In an article called "Here's Another Good Reason Women Should Dump a Toxic Friendship," the *Today* news site highlights research indicating that "as the amount of negativity in relationships increased, [women's] risk of hypertension also increased."

I'm all for reminding women that unhealthy relationships can seriously damage both our bodies and our psyches. But I still must ask, "Isn't there another side to this conversation? Shouldn't we try to figure out how to make stressful relationships less stressful?" We used to say, "Don't fix what isn't broken," but now I feel like we're saying, "Don't even fix what's broken—just get rid of it!" People are not last year's smartphone model to be simply upgraded every year or two.

Relationships Are Worth the Trouble

In her book *Lean In: Women, Work, and the Will to Lead*, Sheryl Sandberg encourages women to keep their feet on the gas pedals of their careers right up to the point of starting a family—as opposed to slowing the car down a hundred miles before the eventual pit stop. She wrote, "We hold ourselves back in ways both big and small . . . by pulling back when we should be leaning in."

The same can be said about friendship. We withdraw when what we actually want—the feeling of safety and connectedness—is just a little farther down the road: on the *other* side of leaning in. Essentially, we need to make sure we've fully leaned in before we decide to pull away. Why? Because, what is worth more trouble than our relationships—what could be more important than contending for love? Wouldn't we want someone to fight for us? And when we say we want people to be "there for us no matter what," don't we include the times when *we're* acting out, being needy, and feeling insecure? If so, why are we tempted to hit the road when our friends do the same with us?

I view my friendships as investments. They are sacred containers where I have stored time, energy, love, memories, and vulnerability. Anyone who has embarked upon a risk-involving venture goes in knowing there will be times when it will be very tempting to just walk away—but we'd only do so *after* we felt we'd done everything we could do to make it work. Relationships, like business, will go through periods of turmoil and low revenue. But we don't just bail in those rough patches; we trust that, with honest accounting and some courageous decisions, we can once again profit from our investment.

It takes a long time to foster a friendship. So when the inevitable disappointments and frustrations show up, I have a commitment to put as much energy into saving the relationship as I've put into developing it. So, if the prospects with a new friend start to look rocky, I probably won't put a ton of energy into saving what may be barely built. But with longtime friends, or intimate and close friends, I am willing to step up, lean in, and give my all to see if we can again find a place of mutual love.

In fact, anytime there is a fight, an unmet need, a slow-boiling frustration, or a repeated judgment in one of our friendships, we have the sacred opportunity to *try* to repair it, develop it, enhance it, and grow it—*before* we end it. To walk away from gaps without trying to close them just leaves a bunch of gaping holes in what could have been full, nurtured hearts. Do we want a cemetery of hurt feelings and friendships that could have been?

Pulling away isn't the path to intimacy. We have to stay loving and curious if we want to get there.

I am willing to put as much energy into the saving *of a friendship as I put into the* development *of that friendship. Pulling away isn't the path to intimacy; we have to stay loving and curious if we want to get there.*

Relationships Are the Gym for Our Personal Growth

Our relationships are the health clubs where we practice intimacy: the places where we build up the muscles of compassion, increase our endurance for sitting with hard feelings, and stretch the flexibility of our biases. It's in our relationships where the rubber meets the road, where we practice being those better people we claim we want to become, the people we wish everyone else could be.

Our greatest selves, our most powerful, loving, generous, strong, happy, and peaceful selves—the selves that can forgive, that are patient, that maintain healthy boundaries—are created only as we practice in our relationships with others. There is no other way. The classrooms where we seek personal growth—whether via creative workshops, religious communities, self-help books, yoga retreats, or therapy sessions—are great for learning technique, teaching us about ourselves, providing ideas, and encouraging a process; until we see ourselves showing up differently with others, we haven't completed the work.

Therefore, our friendships are the gymnasiums for the soul, where we can practice the hard work of relationship, such as:

- Apologizing even when our friends don't.
- Asking our friends what is bothering them even if we're unsure we want to know.
- Brainstorming solutions with our friends to help us love each other in meaningful ways with what we each offer.
- Finding loving ways to say, "I need something different."
- Naming our feelings instead of expecting our friends to guess.
- Practicing empathy even when we're tempted to judge.
- Speaking up honestly even when it's easier to shrug it off and pretend we're fine.
- Releasing our own version of a story instead of looking for more evidence to back it up.
- Staying nondefensive even when we feel attacked.
- Talking to our friend who hurt us instead of complaining about her to everyone else.

Is what I'm encouraging easy? Not at all. Is it awkward? Probably. Stressful? Indeed. Are you unsure how to proceed? I imagine you are.

But let me remind you: When we go to our local health clubs we go with a willingness to sweat and to push ourselves. And when our stamina flags, we might change up our playlists to see if we can find the motivation to run one more hill. When we sign up for a race we do so to feel the weight of a challenge. Whatever regular exercise we commit to, we do it because we know we're better off when we've been on the mat. It's no different with interpersonal exercise. If our goal is to become people who make a difference in this world, then we are called upon to engage with each other and build our emotional muscles.

Some growth will most certainly happen with strangers and acquaintances, but most of our maturation will be with those who are closest to us.

Everyone we're in relationship with will be a teacher to us, with an invitation to see our limits, our judgments, our fears, and our motivations. The more I can see where I am triggered, the more I can practice my internal work: creating greater emotional health in my life. Seeing our friendships as our health clubs not only grows us as individuals—it also increases our chances of moving our friendships into greater intimacy and safety. We aren't likely to reach the peak of the Frientimacy Triangle without sweating through some times when it would have been easier to drift apart.

"I think that we can't go around measuring our goodness by what we don't do: by what we deny ourselves, what we resist, and who we exclude. I think we've got to measure goodness by what we embrace, what we create, and who we include."
—*from* Chocolat

Now, this is not to say that there won't be times when we must end our stressful relationships—or at least establish strong boundaries around them. I'm not against giving women permission to break up; I just encourage us to choose that option as only a last resort, not just when we're tired of putting up with something. Tragically, all too often one woman's "last straw" was the first time the ditched friend even knew there was a problem. So let's lean in before choosing to walk away.

When We Lean In to Relationship, We Lean In to Ourselves

Let's take a look at an example. Two women had been friends for six years. In the course of a few months, they went from being roommates to barely seeing each other because one of them, "Mary Kay," had started working her dream job and no longer felt she had the same time or energy to devote to that friendship. We've been there: moves, new jobs, marriages, divorces, kids, cancer, bankruptcy, starting businesses, empty-nesting, retirement—you name it, our desires and needs can shift. In this case, Mary Kay viewed her friend's continued attempts to invite her out to late night concerts as insensitive of her early morning job. By the time she spoke to me about it, she wanted to end the friendship because she felt her friend was jealous, trying to sabotage her success.

Every change in our lives can impact how we interact. Since major life changes can be hard enough for *us* to transition through with ease, it makes complete sense that those same changes would be disorienting for the people in our lives. As a result, our relationships often need to be renegotiated after change as we all find our footing in the "new normal." When will we see each other, and how often? What will we spend our time talking about, and what moods will we be in at the time? It's no one's fault that as our lives change our friendships must shift as well.

Unfortunately, frequently we don't admit—or aren't even aware—that such renegotiating is taking place. And all too often someone wishes things could go back to how they were, which only complicates the situation, leading to recrimination and tears and statements both later regret—or, worse, silence, with hurt feelings swallowed and ignored as the emotional distance mounts. But our friendships are sacred contracts: We need to renegotiate this unspoken commitment out loud so we can try to figure out what each person needs and preserve what we've built up.

And we don't lean in just for the sake of the friendship. It is here—in this place of friendship disappointment—where we are also invited to grow. Our relationships are mirrors: They show us not just how loved and valuable we are but also where we have room to grow. In fact, since our introspection is limited to that which is conscious, the only way to really know ourselves is through our behaviors and interactions with others. It's only when we face frustration, disappointment, or fear that we can see the areas of growth that are usually subconscious. Our relationships invite us to try new ways of trusting love, healing unexamined narratives, and becoming more compassionate and courageous people. The people in our lives—including our friends—are the path to our personal growth.

Frustration Is a Crucial Part of Every Relationship

Many believe that friendships are supposed to be easy and comfortable: pain free, all fun, total joy. I've heard many quip, "I don't *do* drama" as though they are so enlightened that they can't be bothered with anything that feels messy. But the truth is that conflict and change is part of any healthy relationship, and so we must cease viewing our collisions as bad signs and instead see them as invitations for growth and depth.

In *The Road Less Traveled: A New Psychology of Love, Traditional Values and Spiritual Growth,* psychiatrist M. Scott Peck says, "To fail to confront when confrontation is required"—or offering "thoughtless criticism or condemnation and other forms of *active deprivation of caring*"—"represents a failure to love equally" [the italics are my own]. In other words, while we might claim that our silence is for their good, or to keep the peace, our avoidance can actually withhold the love that every relationship needs.

When we speak of wanting intimacy in romantic relationships, we understand that conflict will be part of the equation. We speak of marriages taking work and aren't shocked when we feel angry at each other at times. However long we may put off the conflict, once we fight and make up we intuitively know the relationship can become safer for us. So why can't we approach our friendships with similar expectations? When hurt, some think they're walking away from the wrong person; I think we all too often walk away from the path to intimacy—which is best learned with the person who has already committed to us rather than with some as yet unknown person who has no commitment to us at all.

Indeed, once we understand just how relationships mature, and that it's only through conflict that we can move into true intimacy, we can see that conflict isn't just *not* to be avoided—it's to be expected, even welcomed.

The Four Stages of Relationships

M. Scott Peck offers additional wisdom in his book *The Different Drum: Community Making and Peace*, which presents four stages of community building that can be just as easily applied to relationships.

The first stage is what he calls PSEUDO-COMMUNITY. This is where we demonstrate our willingness to be friendly and likable. Other psychologists and organizational experts label this stage with words like the "honeymoon period" or "forming," where we tend to avoid discomfort and focus on the positive as we get our bearings in the new relationship.

But notice the name "pseudo-community." *Pseudo* implies that, while it has the appearance of community, it is not genuine community. The point is that we like to think everyone getting along swimmingly *is* intimacy, but we'd be wrong. That's just pleasurable company. True intimacy involves weathering the rough patches, too, finding ways to relate through thick *and* thin.

In the second stage, CHAOS, the façade has faded and we see more clearly the person's imperfections—which then leads to frustration and disappointment, even hurt, as we realize our friend's inability to be exactly what we want. Some organization models call this very normal stage "disintegration" or "storming." In this stage, some will just swallow the hurt and slowly build resentment; others might gradually pull away; and still others might start trying to change the other, whether openly or passive aggressively.

In the EMPTINESS stage it feels worse before it gets better, as we are forced to shed whatever distortions (bias, defensiveness, fear, prejudice, need for power and control) are preventing real communication in the relationship. While Peck calls it an emptying of our preconceived expectations, it is also a type of filling: as we invite empathy, trust, vulnerability, and an open mind into our midst.

Another term I like for this stage is "norming," which is when communication improves as we discuss our expectations, responsibilities, and roles. In this stage, we're hopefully integrating what we know about our friend and her needs with what we want and need. Once we've laid down our swords—along with the stories we've made up about our friend's behaviors—we're able to listen with curiosity and warmth.

Only after these three stages do we experience true community—where we have both consciously adopted complete empathy with each other and a willingness to stay connected. Having related to each other more deeply through the previous stages, we have built a trust that assures we can depend on each other. This stage, called "performing" in the team model, is where the most effectiveness, happiness, and productivity can occur. And in romance, of course, once we reach this stage we believe we can go through anything together.

Far too few friendships reach this stage.

I don't believe we need to go through all these stages with everyone. And even when we do, it doesn't have to be ugly and painful, with shots fired and criticisms launched. But, if we want deeper intimacy in our friendships, then we have to go through the awkwardness of these stages with a few of our friends. And anytime we practice skills that don't come naturally, and that trigger insecurities, we're bound to mess up, say hurtful things, and take things too personally. Like with any new skill, though, it gets easier as we strengthen the muscle.

Learning new skills means a few things: We need to be aware of what new behaviors we want to adopt; we need to accept that it's going to feel awkward for a while; we need to acknowledge that, for a time, we'll likely get it wrong more than we get it right; and we need to be gentle with ourselves as we move toward becoming more proficient. Like a golfer who has to change her swing, it's not going to happen overnight, nor will it feel comfortable or normal. But if we value intimacy, we know it's what we should do for our friendship.

So, let's imagine that we've decided to go to the mat with our friend. How might that look?

The example of Mary Kay, who is weary of her friend's invitations to go to late-night events, is helpful here. Like most of our stories, it isn't some blatant toxicity or cruel conduct that exhausts us as much as it is the meaning we've attached to their behaviors. Because Mary Kay felt frustrated every time her friend reached out—and we tend to want to avoid the scenarios that trigger those feelings—she associated those feelings with the other person and blamed her for her frustration. (I imagine most of us are guilty of having jumped to similar conclusions at some point in our lives.) Indeed, we don't hear Mary Kay's story and scream "Run for your life!" And yet, just hearing her version, describing a "needy friend who either doesn't understand that I have real responsibilities now or doesn't care about my success," then most of us would agree, "Yeah, you don't need that in your life right now!"

But what if Mary Kay chose courageous and loving confrontation before withdrawal, a willingness to lean in before pulling away? Instead of blaming her friend and taking her actions personally, what if she were to pause long enough to ask, *"Why do I really feel frustrated? What if this incident to me represents something bigger; and, if so, what does it represent? What is actually causing my feelings? What is it that I need?"* Were Mary Kay willing to do this—were she even to know that she *could* do this—then maybe, just maybe, that friendship could not only be saved but also actually deepened. If she were able to name what was really bothering her—feeling like her friend didn't respect her job, feeling bad because she always says "no"— then she could start to see where a conversation might bring more awareness to their friendship.

To follow are four actions we can engage in when we choose to discuss our frustration or hurt. Note, though, that in every confrontation the goal isn't for us to feel better by dumping our feelings on the other; rather our goal is to deepen the intimacy by inviting conversation. We want to open up space with questions, not shut it down with blame.

EXPRESSING LOVE: Every conflict that can start with love helps remind both people that the goal is greater connection, not less. For example, "It's because I love you and want our relationship healthy that I'm bringing this up," or, "I am so grateful for how long we've been friends—I hope that's always the case."

VALIDATING FEELINGS: It makes sense that we feel loss or disappointment when there's conflict. But remember that we're not the only ones feeling that disappointment. Always try to find out what your friend is feeling—and assure her that you can understand how yucky that would feel. For better or for worse, all feelings are valid, whether we agree with them or not. Offer her precisely what you'd like from her: the loving empathy of someone who cares how the other feels, regardless of the details. (It so happens that just hearing one's feelings being validated—in other words, just feeling heard— can greatly calm hurt feelings, so the practice can actually help both of you.)

REMOVING BLAME: Your ego wants to come out of this declaring you the winner—but you've got to let that go. Love means that both people will win; conflict resolution means both people are satisfied with the result. This isn't about who was right—it's about practicing love.

REQUESTING WILLINGNESS: You don't have to have a solution at the ready. All you have to know is that you want to try to repair it, and you're inviting her to be a part of that process with you. You can do this with questions like, "I feel like there's some tension between us. Would you be willing to talk about it?" or, "Okay, so you feel X and I feel Y. What can we do to help us both feel better?"

If we apply the above steps to Mary Kay's scenario, what possibilities might open up between them? Perhaps instead of just declining her friend's invitations, Mary Kay could offer an alternative: "I always feel so bad when you invite me and I can't go. It's not that I don't want to be with you; it's just that my new job is so important to me and requires me to wake up early.

Are there other times we can hang out?" In that statement she expresses her love in her desire to connect, acknowledges that the current invitations don't feel good, avoids any statements of blame, and states her willingness to find other times to be with her.

Or, if Mary Kay really does feel her friend is trying to sabotage her, isn't it worth her asking before walking away? She could say, "I've started feeling like you don't care about my job, which feels awful since I love it so much. It's entirely possible I've misread that though, so I wanted to check in with you to see if there's anything we need to talk through about how this job has impacted our friendship. Because I really value you." This approach shows how much she desires a healthy future for the friendship, states very clearly how she's interpreting the behavior, demonstrates her willingness to own that interpretation, and opens a dialogue for her friend to respond.

As is true in any case, it could just as easily be the other friend who bravely reaches out to start the conversation. What if the inviting friend is hurt that *she's* the one always inviting Mary Kay, who always declines? What if, instead of taking it personally, or deciding that a friend who never puts forth any effort isn't worth it, she were to say, "I miss you so much and wish we could spend time together. But since I've repeatedly invited you out and you're never able to come, I'm starting to feel like you don't want to spend time with me. I wanted to check in with you in case you were just really busy or if there was something that was bothering you." With this she openly shares her feelings, resists the desire to make judging and blaming statements, shows she values the friendship, and ends with a query that invites deeper conversation. Can you feel a little bit of space opening up in this friendship by one of them courageously leaning in?

When It's Not Working

I choose to play the odds that leaning in *could* improve every friendship. Not that it always will, but that it always could. Unfortunately though, while many relationships recover and even strengthen from both parties leaning in, not every friendship grows deeper. In such situations, ideally one of the following two outcomes could be managed, as each is still preferable to simply walking away entirely.

1. FIND PEACE WITH LESS: Just because two people can't be as close as they once were—for whatever reason—it doesn't mean they can't remain connected. It can still be enjoyable to keep in touch, meeting up every now and then. Most of all, friends can remain open to the idea that, as life continues to change, they might find their paths can again mesh in meaningful ways. It doesn't have to be all or nothing, a "ten" or a "zero." Allowing some friends to shift to something in between is usually still worth the effort.

2. CRAFT A HEALTHY CLOSURE: Let's say two friends have talked about their feelings, and understand where each other is coming from, but the only accord they can reach is to acknowledge the drift in the relationship. Ideally they can create a healthy closure to the friendship in the same way that a romantic couple might part amicably. This is important because when we end a friendship without striving for healthy closure, we prevent ourselves from learning and growing—and we complicate our grief with unknowing. Furthermore, we set ourselves up for repeating a similar situation with *other* friends. It's far better to learn friendship skills with the friends we already have.

But no matter what the outcome, ideally with every relationship, when we practice taking initiative and taking responsibility, we can say that we showed up and we tried. In doing so, we build strong emotional muscles. That means that with each effort we can better learn how to take things less personally, how to empathize more deeply, even how to forgive. Our relationship aptitude expands when our experience increases. The more we practice, the more successful we can become in finding joy in all our relationships.

Leaning in to intimacy is not a road of weakness but one of strength—a journey not for the faint of heart but for the deep of heart. What I am calling you to is the work of a super heroine: the path of courage, kindness, and strength. It's how you can become more loving—and attract more loving people into your life.

Worth Remembering

- Anytime there is a fight, an unmet need, a slow-boiling frustration, or a repeated judgment in one of our friendships, we have the sacred opportunity to try to repair it, develop it, enhance it, and grow it—before we end it.

- If our goal is to become people who make a difference in this world, then we are called upon to engage with each other and build our emotional muscles.

- Once we understand just how relationships mature, and that it's only through conflict that we can move into true intimacy, we can see that conflict isn't just *not* to be avoided—it's to be expected, even welcomed.

- We can work to heal rifts and deepen intimacy in our friendships by expressing love, validating feelings, removing blame, and requesting willingness.

- Though not all friendships can be saved, ideally with every relationship we practice taking initiative and taking responsibility, all with honesty and heart.

Next up: when believing we're not good enough limits the intimacy in our lives.

9

Obstacle to Intimacy #1: Doubting Our Self-Worth

Or: The Fear *We're* Not Good Enough

started GirlFriendCircles.com in 2008 with two competing feelings: idealism for introducing women to new friends, and insecurity that I wasn't capable of doing it. Who was I to start a business without an MBA, a savings account, or any experience in technology? My new business cards were emblazoned with CEO of GirlFriendCircles.com only because that sounded more impressive than the truth: Girl Who Sits at Her Computer in Yoga Pants Hoping Her Idea Works Someday.

And nothing triggered my insecurity more than attending networking events or business conferences surrounded by people who looked like they knew what they were doing and knew how to do it. So I was frequently tempted to look confident and focus my conversations on the early PR wins and the success stories women had shared. When at times I thought I'd impressed a fellow attendee, for a brief moment I'd feel a bit more like I belonged. But then I'd just as quickly feel like a fraud, knowing deep down that I wasn't one of them: I didn't know the right people, pick the best business model, or understand all the terms being thrown around. It was really a no-win situation: If they weren't impressed it validated my insecurity, but if they were impressed, I worried I'd given the wrong impression.

To this day, the moments when I feel most insecure are still the times I worry most about what everyone is thinking of me. But the thing is, it's tiring enough just managing my life; trying to also manage everyone's impression of me is downright exhausting. It's a dangerous trap to believe we need to wow others in order to be loved. It's dangerous because it does more than risk our never feeling loved for who we are—it also lessens the chances of actual relating and connecting deeply with others.

The trap of "wowing" can play out in different ways. Some link their value to serving others or to being needed. Others equate value in being right, and, if their ideas or beliefs are questioned, they can feel their very core is threatened. Some most fear being seen as needy or vulnerable, so they feel loved only when they are seen as strong. Others need to be seen as highly competent and poised—in a word: perfect. And some fear they're liked only if they're fun and energetic, heartfelt laughter always at the ready.

But while what we think we need in order to be liked can be part of who we are, none of that paves the path to intimacy. Intimacy eventually asks us to risk believing that we are lovable even when we're not performing, or when we don't come across as amazing, knowledgeable, or strong. In short, fear that we aren't good enough blocks us from deepening intimacy.

GENTLE TRUTH: We can't enjoy intimacy if we don't like ourselves

This chapter might at first sound similar to the next chapter, which discusses the fear of rejection. And perhaps the two fears are two sides of the same coin. But I distinguish the fear of rejection as worrying about not being liked by others; whereas when we doubt our self-worth the fear is that we don't even like ourselves. My illustration above was about my own suffering from imposter syndrome, not anyone else putting that on me. Indeed, why wait for others to reject us when we can just beat them to the punch?

So we start with this fear because it resides in the core of every other fear. Any healthy relationship practices we might engage in must be built on the foundation that we *know* we're valuable and worthy of being in meaningful relationships. If encouraging you to be more consistent or vulnerable triggers fears that you aren't good enough or lovable enough for others to value, then that encouragement could seem like an impossible request. But fortunately such doesn't indicate a dead end. That's because our relationships don't just increase the love in our lives—they also serve as the training center for practicing our most important relationship of all: the one with ourselves. It's a promise that, as we practice extending love to ourselves more, it'll gradually become easier for us to courageously reveal ourselves to others, too.

If I were to ask you if you love yourself more now than you did five years ago, how would you answer? Would you be able to point to evidence that you treat yourself better? That you let yourself rebound from disappointment faster? That you are more comfortable with your success and power? That you're willing to forgive yourself faster rather than beat yourself up? Answering yes to any of these questions suggests you are developing self-worth.

Far too many of us take our relationship with ourselves for granted. But be clear, just as intimacy with others doesn't *just* happen, neither does intimacy with ourselves. Nor should we think we're the only ones harmed if we don't attend to loving ourselves; the truth is that self-neglect hurts all our relationships.

One woman I know apologizes all the time. Like. All. The. Time. She thinks everything she does is wrong or, at best, could have been done better. A friend of mine is plagued with regret after most social situations, beating herself up for what she "should" have said and then doubting that others like her. One friend confided to me that it's sometimes hard for her to listen to others because she's so worried about what she's going to say when it's her turn. And another friend seems unable to accept how much her friends really love her, and repeatedly needs them to prove it.

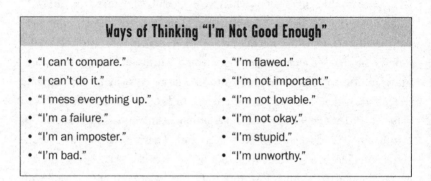

Ways of Thinking "I'm Not Good Enough"

- "I can't compare."
- "I can't do it."
- "I mess everything up."
- "I'm a failure."
- "I'm an imposter."
- "I'm bad."
- "I'm flawed."
- "I'm not important."
- "I'm not lovable."
- "I'm not okay."
- "I'm stupid."
- "I'm unworthy."

We all know the accusing inner voice that tells us we're not good enough. We know the insecurities of wondering if we fit in or are liked, the tendency to take things personally, the desire to feel chosen and special, the need to have others validate us before we can feel safe. We know the temptation to rehash conversations and events, perpetually asking, "Why didn't I say such-and-such instead?" Whether all this sounds like either that cartoon devil on one shoulder telling you how bad you are, or the little angel on the other sweetly noting you could be better—either way, both pitchforks and halos can leave us feeling inadequate.

"One of the most prevalent reasons women are unhappy, unfulfilled, and stressed-out is the mental and emotional abuse suffered at their own hands." This text comes from the book *Reform Your Inner Mean Girl: 7 Steps to Stop Bullying Yourself and Start Loving Yourself,* by Amy Ahlers and Christine Arylo. In fact, they've named thirteen types of Inner Mean Girls—including the Worrywart, the Doing Addict, the Invincible Super-woman, and the Martyr—whose voices unfortunately sound all too familiar to most of us. We all say things to ourselves and about ourselves that we, hopefully, would never say to a friend.

The shortage of self-confidence for females in particular is well quantified and documented. Repeated studies have demonstrated that, while men tend to overestimate their abilities and performance, women underestimate both. On the subject of women's low confidence, an article in *The Atlantic* concluded, "Women feel confident only when they are perfect." Wow—nothing like setting a high bar!

Science reveals that feelings of self-value aren't based on actual fact—on the external circumstances—but on how *we* perceive those circumstances. My girlfriend who has a hard time trusting that her friends *really* like her is evidence that it doesn't matter what we think about her—she sees herself differently. That's how women many see as gorgeous can never feel pretty enough, loving and generous mothers question whether they're good moms, and dedicated, successful career women can believe they don't work hard enough.

Call it self-respect, self-love, or self-worth; by any name, the idea is that we need to intrinsically *know* that we are good, valuable, and worthy. And so it's not that we need to change the external circumstances; it's that we need to change our perceptions.

Sometimes it's not that we need better friends, a better us, or better situations—but rather we need to believe what is already true.

Abandoning Ourselves

Many self-help experts insist "Others can't love you more than you love yourself," or "You have to love yourself before others can love you."

I don't agree with those statements. I believe it's possible for people to love you more than you can absorb. I also know that being loved by another can create the space for you to love yourself better. But at the end of the day, loving ourselves *is* an inside job. It doesn't *have* to start with you, but it's still your responsibility to do whatever you can to know your own self-worth. Much the way someone can't burn our calories for us, we can't just wait to feel loveable only when someone chooses us and tells us we're loveable.

"I've discovered that there really is one major cause of relationship problems—one issue that if you address and heal, everything changes," promises Dr. Margaret Paul, a well-known relationship counselor whose nearly five decades of working with couples can benefit us in the platonic world as well.

Her answer? Self-abandonment.

The Encarta World English Dictionary defines *abandon* as "to leave somebody or something behind for others to look after, especially somebody or something meant to be a personal responsibility." In other words, we abandon ourselves when we relinquish to others how we feel about ourselves, judging ourselves through others' eyes, ignoring or dismissing our own feelings, or manipulating others into feeling guilty for how "they" made us feel. But we are not worthy *only* when others say we are, loveable only when told we are, or valuable only when treated as such. We are those things—regardless of the actions or commitments of others.

If we've basically abandoned ourselves, and can't believe in the love others give us, any practice we do to increase the intimacy and love in our lives would be moot. If we go through life believing it's *their* job to make us feel loved, we in effect show up with a bucket that leaks.

Think of every friendship you build as a well that you dig together, and its water as the love you give to each other. If we're going to go through the hard work of digging a well, it would be wise to make sure our containers can hold the water we draw from it. So we'll want to find the leaks in our buckets and patch them as best we can. We also have to recognize love when it's coming to us—so we can hold out our bucket to receive it. We have to believe we are lovable so that all our kind actions come not out of insecurities and manipulation, but out of real love. We have to know our value so deeply that we're not afraid to look at ourselves and take responsibility for how we contributed to the issue by responding out of fear or anger or shame, instead of compassion.

What Do Leaks Sound Like?

- "I doubt she'll ever be able to see the real me."
- "I must be defective; I can't seem to do anything right."
- "I must stay happy and upbeat so she'll want to be my friend!"
- "If only I hadn't shown her my feelings everything would be okay."
- "If she really knew how crazy some of my thoughts are, she'd never want to be my friend."
- "What if I say the wrong thing? Or don't do what she's expecting?"
- "What if she doesn't really admire me? What if she doesn't even like me?"

When we feel small, some of us puff up and push our way in, some shrink and shrivel, and some try to earn and manipulate. In an ideal world we'd all stand secure in our worth, never doubting. But even when we can achieve that confidence, we'll still fall off balance at times, likely defaulting to our old ways just to remind ourselves we're okay. And it certainly doesn't help that our human tendency is to feel we lack something—and then to focus on that. When we add to the mix a capitalist world that earns fortunes convincing us of the same thing, it's no wonder we're left feeling everyone else got the secret password to life except us.

So yes, we are engaging in this practice together so as to learn to be a great friend to others, but in order to do so we also have to be a best friend to ourselves.

Self-Worth Isn't Narcissism

As we each try to become more comfortable with our power, our potential, and our greatness, we risk bumping up against our fear of arrogance. And it's true that moving the pendulum from false humility to self-confidence can feel a bit like bragging. But it's crucial to realize that loving ourselves isn't bragging. Bragging roars with a need to intimidate, even with a bullying stance. Arrogance implies superiority, a need to be above others. Honestly, I've met few women who even come close to that.

We're so afraid of the far extreme that most of us dare not move closer to the center. We're so afraid of pretentious bravado that we're not even being brave. But while we might fear becoming conceited and vain, it's actually false arrogance we should be afraid of—boasting because we *don't* feel worthy. A low self-worth can manifest as grandiosity or condemnation; self-worth looks more like peace.

Self-worth is coming to peace with who we are such that we're willing to share our gift in this world. And keep in mind, knowing ourselves so well that we can name our gifts is nowhere close to thinking we're above others, and neither does it bring with it a need to push others down. Self-worth simply recognizes that we, like others, have value.

Why is that so hard? Because we live in a world that, unfortunately, values certain skills, appearances, and achievements above others, as deemed by the sense of importance and value of our culture. And often that hierarchy of significance is upside down. When we buy into it, our own sense of value and worth becomes upside down, too.

Consider the human body metaphor, we are all a different part, and each isn't just important—it's essential. And every part is interdependent with the other parts. Or recall the cartoon in chapter 5, the bird, monkey, penguin, elephant, goldfish, seal, and dog are equally talented and valuable—for their function, within their environment. Ideally we, too, can acknowledge how we all have a different purpose, be thrilled to be what we are, and then desire to be the best of it we can be.

In my experience the more people know their worth, the more they can see it in others, and the more they want to serve the world. So the more people see how special they are, the more they see how special everyone is.

COURAGEOUS ACTIONS: Three Practices for Being Our Own Best Friend

We can grow weary if those close to us keep asking, "Are you sure you love me?" We *want* the people who love us to know it, to feel it, and to believe it. So then wouldn't we want the same in our relationship with ourselves?

Our goal is to get to a place where the love we receive from others adds to, and mirrors, the love we have for ourselves. I invite you to trust that you will be a bigger gift to everyone else the more you know what makes you unique, the more you can articulate your value, and the more you can be comfortable with all your feelings. To follow are three practices to help you do these things.

Practice #1: Know Who You Are

To love ourselves, we have to accept ourselves. And to accept ourselves, we have to know ourselves.

To know ourselves we have to be willing to truly look at ourselves, willing to perceive the good, the bad, and the ugly *before* we can conclude that we are worthy of love from ourselves and others—and, from that love, conclude we have a beautiful contribution to make in this world.

In her book *Madly in Love with Me,* Christine Arylo says: "People often ask me, 'What is the first step in loving yourself?' And while the execution isn't always simple, the answer . . . is." She says that after making the choice to want to love yourself, "The next step is knowing who you *really* are behind all the ideas, masks, personas, ideals, layers of protections, and societal and familial baggage."

That means that knowing ourselves doesn't mean simply deciding what career makes us happy, what style of clothing feels right for us, or how we prefer to spend our weekends. Those are certainly good beginnings, but are you truly willing to be curious and introspective about yourself? For example, consider the following questions:

Resources For Getting to Know You and Your Friends

The contents of these books and resources, while designed for your personal growth, could also make for a stimulating book club selection, a meaningful activity on a girls' weekend away, an invitation to bond with a friend—or even just a casual conversation over drinks.

ENNEAGRAM: This is by far my favorite personal growth system. It not only provides vocabulary for how my subconscious actually makes decisions, it also shares information about how to grow into a healthier and more integrated expression of who we each are. It's pretty layered and deep, so I recommend utilizing the book *The Wisdom of the Enneagram* by Don Riso and Russ Hudson to help you really dive in. You can take a free test to help determine what type you are at www.enneagraminstitute.com/guide-to-all-riso-hudson-tests. I highly recommend reading through the top few possibilities to see which type resonates the most with you.

STRENGTHSFINDER: This powerful tool helps us realize our natural strengths and talents—so we can spend more of our life doing the things that energize us. The $10 online test takes about fifteen to twenty minutes to complete and the results are easy to share and understand. But the "real" test comes with integrating the information into our lives! (www.gallupstrengthscenter.com)

MYERS-BRIGGS: This is an old standby, one of the most well-known temperament sorters, so tests abound online. Like with StrengthsFinder, it's important to apply the inventory learned in order to understand how that makes us truly different from those with whom we're in relationships. (My personal favorite source for the latter is David Keirsey's *Please Understand Me II: Temperament, Character, Intelligence*; my copy is marked-up and dog-eared from nearly two decades of use!)

LOVE LANGUAGES: Many of us, if asked to name what makes us feel loved—words of affirmation, physical touch, acts of service, meaningful gifts, or quality time—could identify our preferences from the list; others wouldn't necessarily know how to answer if unprompted. That being the case, spending time with friends talking about how we feel most loved can provide amazing awareness into how we can best communicate our affection. A helpful guide in this is Gary Chapman's book *The Five Love Languages: How to Express Heartfelt Commitment to Your Mate*. It's a quick read and is as applicable with family as it is with friends. (You can take the quiz at www.5lovelanguages.com.)

MADLY IN LOVE WITH ME: This book was written by my friend Christine Arylo. In it she guides women to identify which of the ten branches in our personal Self-Love Tree—such as self-expression, self-care, or self-forgiveness— might need our love and attention in order to blossom. The book includes guided meditations, worksheets, and book discussion questions all ready for you to determine how you can become your own best friend. (www.madlyinlovewithme.com)

- Can you articulate how your life experiences have uniquely shaped you?
- Do you know what energizes you and drains you—what tasks, what people, what conversations?
- Do you know what message you subconsciously go through life hoping to hear from others?
- Do you know what values are really guiding your life?
- Do you know with what you're most likely to get defensive and feel threatened?
- Do you know who you are at your core—where even if you lost your job, marriage, and home you could still describe who you are?
- Do you understand how your temperament is different from that of others?
- What makes you special?

An additional question, if you do know who you are, are you becoming more comfortable with expressing it? Or, if not yet, do you think you'd be open to getting more comfortable expressing it?

I find that many women who create art are hesitant to use the word "artist" if they've never made money from their creations, but artists they are nonetheless. Many women feel narcissistic to admit they feel beautiful—even if they think it secretly—but hiding it makes it no less true. Why can't we acknowledge when we feel pretty? Many women feel scared to admit how ambitious they feel, fearful it makes them unrelatable, but their drive is there all the same. We downplay our talents, our gifts, our accomplishments, our callings, our desires, and our greatness like kids playing whack-a-mole at the arcade, scared that to show our faces above ground might make us unlikable.

As a participant in a workshop designed to help us articulate our essence—the unique energy or expression that we each exude—I kept trying to find softer words to describe one of the two metaphors that emerged as my core being. It felt presumptuous to say, "I am fire," so I kept trying on variations like "I am *like* a fire . . . I am a campfire . . . I am an inviting fire . . . I am a safe fire . . ." The facilitator kept pushing me: "Why are you so afraid to be fire?" to which I responded, "It just feels so big. Who am I to be fire? I don't want to scare people." She was graciously relentless. "Shasta—you *are* fire. Not saying it doesn't make it not so—it just weakens your awareness of what you're called to do in this world."

Friendspiration: "I desire knowing myself so well that
I feel better sharing myself with others."

It's important to practice owning our strengths and celebrating our lives, and it's among friends with whom we feel safe that we can do so. One way we can practice is by trying on phrases that might otherwise sound pretentious. So let's whisper our secret hopes to, try on big ideas with, and practice celebrating our contributions among those we love, and who love us.

And as we learn more about who we are, the additional bonus is that our friends get to know us better, too. Working through inventories, workshops, and books together can be a huge boost to friendships because these resources provide everyone a structure to step into. They can also provide a vocabulary for our differences—all of which helps us to see ourselves and our friends more clearly.

FOR REFLECTION: Write out your answers to the bullet-list questions above.

FOR PRACTICE: Consider exploring one or more of the self-knowledge resources in the "Resources" sidebar on page 150—especially if you do so with friends!

I have retrained my brain to believe that there is a beautiful core to me that is safe, unchanging, undamaged, and perfect. But I didn't always believe that.

Few of us get through childhood without developing the limiting belief that we aren't good enough. Given that I was raised in a Christian denomination that talks a lot about sin, I heard that I was born a lowly sinner—and that, while God was love, we didn't deserve that love. And so though the belief that there was a spark of perfect and innocent love in me may have flickered at times, the light was dimmed by the shame of my unworthiness.

Fortunately, my continued spiritual journey eventually brought me to understand grace, and to see that I was made in the image of God. And there was nothing—no mistake, no abuse, no experience, no loss—that could extinguish the spark of love in me. I may not always live from that place of compassion and love, but it is there, it is good, it is accessible, and it is safe—no matter what I've survived, how broken I feel, how scared I can be, or how many people reject me. The Christian Scriptures attest, "Not even death can separate us from that love." If God can love me that much, then surely I can try to do the same. Another verse we often hear is "Love your neighbor *as* yourself." But while we have a long way to go in actually loving our neighbors well, most Christians unfortunately skip right over the part about loving ourselves.

The details of why *you* may feel unworthy probably differ from mine, but the truth is that far too many people don't grow up believing they deserve to be loved unconditionally, perfectly, and equally. Whatever your worldview, I hope it encompasses the belief that nobody's opinion of you changes who you actually are. To know the part of you that is pure and loveable is part of the work of this lifetime; for the more we know what is good in us, the more we know how to gift the world with it.

The more you have felt ostracized, the more hidden you may feel. Perhaps you built a castle around your heart, a barrier to protect what felt fragile. If so, I honor that in you, knowing you likely did the best you could do to protect what felt significant. But, assuming you're not currently experiencing trauma and onslaught, I can assure you that safety isn't to be found by forever hiding behind a stone wall. At some point a stone wall can't save us from our own diminishing words and actions, and only serves to remind us that we aren't free. We have to come out from behind our walls.

Friendspiration: "There is a safe piece of me that is pure, innocent, good, and worthy."

Easier said than done, I know. But few practices will change your life more than knowing that your value doesn't rise and fall on how others respond to you. In an extreme example, even someone wanting to abuse you or kill you for who you are wouldn't make you wrong; it may, like for Martin Luther King Jr. and thousands of other bright lights in this world, simply mean that you are indeed the blessing you're intended to be. Fortunately, the level of rejection most of us will know will be more benign: unanswered calls and emails, cutting remarks, jobs we weren't given, parties we weren't invited to. Those are our practice fields—our venues where we practice reminding ourselves of our real worth.

Knowing our worth doesn't mean we don't feel the sting—we will. But, knowing in our hearts what it is about us that is good and beautiful and innocent will ensure that we recover faster, and will feel less inclined to hang on to—or spread—the hurt.

FOR REFLECTION: Journal about a memory when you felt pure, innocent, good, and worthy. How old were you? What were you doing? What do you associate with helping you feel your value?

FOR PRACTICE: Dr. Christiane Northrup, a prolific author on women's health and aging, insists that learning to recognize our value must be the foundation of whatever healthy practices we adopt. She challenges women to, for a month, look deep into their eyes in the mirror every morning and say: "I really, really love you." Though it will feel uncomfortable for the first few weeks, she promises that in time something shifts, and we begin to transform the disparaging looped messages we've been listening to in our heads—essentially recording over the old tape the new message our soul needs to hear.

Practice #3: Know What You're Feeling

Many a friendship goes awry because we don't feel like the other person *gets* us—what it's like to be a mom, to lose someone we love, to end a relationship, to not have enough money, to have chronic pain, to have an abusive parent. But before we blame those who "don't know" us, the question is ours: "Do I even know what I'm feeling? If so, am I communicating it as clearly as possible?"

And while some circumstances seem to employ obvious feelings, how often do you walk around with unrecognized tension in your shoulders or a pit in your stomach? How often do you feel stupid for feeling sensitive, worried, or embarrassed, so you try to stuff it down and tell it to go away? How often do you answer, "I'm fine" or "It's nothing" after a sincere inquiry made by someone you love?

I posit that, more often than we are aware, we can't articulate what exactly is causing us to act out in frustration, shut down in fear, eat in denial, or pour ourselves absentmindedly into work. We are often simply too busy—or too scared—to actually stop and identify *why* we feel what we feel. Most of us avoid our feelings, for many reasons. But to discount our feelings robs us of the self-awareness that helps us to identify what is wrong. How can we attend to something we can't recognize for what it is? And how can we improve our chances of being understood by others if we lack the ability to communicate our feelings even to ourselves?

In *Emotional Intelligence 2.0* Dr. Travis Bradberry and Jean Greaves, drawing conclusions from having tested over half a million people, claim that only 36 percent of us are able to accurately identify our emotions as they happen. There is a "global deficit in understanding and managing emotions." That means that nearly two-thirds of us go through life on auto-pilot, controlled by feelings without awareness.

While lack of self-awareness can involve unnamed emotions, it can also involve misnamed emotions. For example, brain function specialist Dr. Arlene Taylor observes that women have a tendency to misidentify their feelings of anger as sadness. Men, interestingly, are the opposite—they are more likely to express anger when they are actually sad. While these patterns aren't too surprising given where our culture has come from, I hope this default is changing, especially as we parent a new generation of boys told it's okay to cry and girls told it's okay to be angry. Given that sadness is the healthy response to loss, and anger is the healthy response to violated boundaries, to misidentify each can result in confusion as to what actions might improve whatever situation we find ourselves in. Violated boundaries call for standing up and claiming space, not for withdrawing in tears. "Many women are on antidepressants," Dr. Taylor says, "not because they're sad, but because they are angry."

A woman once described an incident that triggered her frustration with her husband. "I just need to get over it," she said, shaking her head. She felt guilty for feeling frustrated. I wished instead that she had felt curious, because I believe her body was trying to tell her that something mattered to her. That frustration was a messenger identifying a need that wasn't being met. To brush off any feeling doesn't make its source disappear—it only prevents us from hearing our inner wisdom.

Similarly, psychiatrist Julie Holland wrote an op-ed in *The New York Times* about a woman who wanted to raise her antidepressant dose. Why? Because she was so mad at her boss she couldn't get her work done. But the problem wasn't her feelings—it was that she wasn't listening to them, mining them for understanding. If we deny our feelings, how can we respond to them in healthy and constructive ways?

Dr. Holland had more to say about how women especially tend to over-medicate their feelings:

Gathering Information from Our Feelings

An advocate for being brave enough to be vulnerable, author Brené Brown says: "Authenticity is a collection of choices that we have to make every day. It's about the choice to show up and be real. The choice to be honest. The choice to let our true selves be seen."

To do this, we need to name what we're feeling with far greater accuracy and nuance than most of us take the time to do. From there, we'd be wise to stay with that feeling long enough to inquire of ourselves:

- What incident prompted this feeling?
- What is it about that incident that triggers this feeling for me? What does it symbolize or communicate to me?
- What exactly am I feeling?
- What information is there for me in this moment? What do I need to know?
- Is there an action I need to take that might help me eventually feel peace again?

It's a valuable exercise to retrain our brains to not deny or squash our emotions. To instead actually identify what we're feeling and intentionally choose how we want to respond is the work of maturity.

To help you in that practice, you can download this feelings inventory (www.cnvc.org/Training/feelings-inventory) to your computer or phone. Then, anytime you feel triggered by an emotion, make it a habit to review the feelings to identify what best captures exactly how you're feeling. Once armed with this information you can then make wiser choices on how you want to respond.

Women's emotionality is a sign of health, not disease; it is a source of power. But we are under constant pressure to restrain our emotional lives. We have been taught to apologize for our tears, to suppress our anger, and to fear being called hysterical.

She reports that one in four women in America now takes a psychiatric medication—even though the vast majority of those diagnosed with depression don't meet the clinical criteria. In her book *Moody Bitches: The Truth About the Drugs You're Taking, The Sleep You're Missing, the Sex You're Not*

Having, and What's Really Making You Crazy, she makes the strong case that we overmedicate because we're uncomfortable with what we're feeling, and too often opt for the easy route instead of dealing with the issues provoking our feelings. She pleads for us to "stop labeling our sadness and anxiety as uncomfortable symptoms, and to appreciate them as a healthy, adaptive part of our biology." This isn't to say that medications aren't helpful and necessary, in many situations they certainly can be. This is to say that we don't want to use them as a substitute for the hard work of identifying the source of our feelings and learning how to act in ways that will empower our lives.

Friendspiration: "My feelings are messengers of
wisdom guiding me back to contentment."

Emotional Intelligence (EQ) can be summed up by our ability to correctly identify our feelings—and then to know what to do with that information so as to restore our equanimity. As such, healthy women will want to become practiced at efficiently determining what they're feeling and why. Ideally we'd be familiar with our sadness (knowing whether it's despair, melancholy, or disappointment, for example) and our anger (whether it's dismay, impatience, or rage). Ideally we'd be committed to not just processing any catalyzing event but also learning the coping skills for returning to a place of peace. Our goal isn't to deny feelings, or numb ourselves when "inconvenient" feelings show up; our goal is to trust our feelings as messengers of information that give us wisdom.

Girlfriends, we are responsible for knowing how we feel. Let's get in touch with ourselves, and trust that our emotions are trying to convey the wisdom we need. And the benefit doesn't end there. Identifying what we're feeling improves our friendships—if others can empathize with us (which necessitates that we've clearly communicated our feelings!), they can ultimately create a bond with us.

FOR REFLECTION: Download the feelings inventory mentioned in the Gathering Information from Our Feelings sidebar on page 153. As practice for naming your feelings, circle the three to five words (or add others!) that you'd use to describe how you feel about your life right now.

FOR PRACTICE: Since speaking our feelings takes getting used to, I've found it helpful to practice in less emotional relationships, like with our server at a restaurant or with our hairdresser. Too often we don't speak up when our food order isn't right or when we're worried about how much hair is getting cut. Think of ways you can express similar concerns in a kind and constructive manner—and then practice them.

Imperfection Is More Than Okay

So now, let's bring the discussion back to how the fear of insufficiency reduces our chances of building intimacy. Those fears are holes in our love buckets; your job, like mine, is to identify, and then work to heal, the holes that leak the love in our buckets. To do that we will want to step into all three of these powerful actions:

- Choosing to really get to know yourself more and more. This means finding language to describe how valuable you are, and not judging yourself so harshly for your flaws.

- Trusting that there is a part of you that is beautiful, lovable, and truly good.

- Becoming more comfortable with listening to your feelings instead of brushing them off, disparaging them, or ignoring them.

And let's also be clear: It's entirely possible the vast majority of us will never heal *all* our holes, and that's okay, too. The goal isn't perfection, but growth.

To revisit my journey with GirlFriendCircles.com, I may never lose the initial desire to impress people—that may be a hole that stays with me. I may rarely walk into a business conference feeling peace rather than insecurity. But I certainly can increase my awareness. Otherwise, if the need to impress went unchecked I'd be tempted to appear successful and dazzling—which could distract me from asking questions, listening, and seeking the help of others. Essentially, my unchecked need could jeopardize the opportunity to forge the connections I most want.

Now that I have increased my awareness, I know I don't need to prove myself to a room of strangers; I know my value is stable, my worth constant. I neither need to puff up nor shrink; rather, I just need to show up and relate.

One of my favorite stories is that of the Indian *bishti*, or water-carrier, whose job it was to fill two large pots of water—one at each end of a pole carried across his shoulders—and haul them to his village every day. One pot never lost its water, but the other pot had a crack, from which trickled half its water on each trip home.

After a while, the pot that leaked its water felt such shame that he apologized to his master for failing to live up to expectations. The water-bearer told the pot to admire the beautiful flowers along one side of the path. Aware of the leaking, the man had planted seeds on the side that got watered during every trip home, thus gifting the entire community with their blooms.

We can be broken and cracked and still experience intimacy. We are worthy of being loved and are capable of loving—no matter how many leaks we have. We may always have wounds that cause us to shrink, feelings that we deny, fears that diminish our self-confidence, or fractures that keep us from holding all the love we receive. So let us acknowledge that—and hope that something beautiful can spring up from whatever drips out.

In telling that story, I don't subscribe to the view that people are "broken." Rather, there are some people who are simply more awake to who they really are. Yes, some people are asleep to their value, and that can cause them to act out in unhealthy ways, but take heart: All of us are in the process of waking up. And with every realization, we can learn and heal and accept ourselves more fully—trusting that we're loveable no matter what.

Worth Remembering

- Fear that we aren't good enough stands in the way of deepening intimacy.

- Just as intimacy with others doesn't *just* happen, neither does intimacy with ourselves. And being a best friend to ourselves correlates to our ability to befriend others.

- Loving ourselves is an inside job. If we go through life believing it's the job of others to make us feel loved, we in effect show up to our relationships with a bucket that leaks.

- Self-worth isn't bragging; self-worth is coming to peace with who we are such that we're willing to share our gift in this world.

- Self-worth comes from knowing who we are, knowing our value, and knowing our feelings.

- Self-worth also comes from accepting our imperfections. Know that most of us won't heal all our holes, and that's okay; our goal isn't perfection, but growth.

Next up: how fear of being rejected hampers our efforts toward frientimacy.

10

Obstacle to Intimacy #2: The Fear of Rejection

Or, The Fear *They* Don't Think We're Good Enough

U gh, you won't believe this," my girlfriend Daneen told me with dismay in her voice, "but Lily came home and cried because she felt left out at school today. Any chance you have friendship workshops for kids?" she asked, somewhat rhetorically.

The experience of feeling left out is certainly one we all know too well—no surprise there. The part of the story that felt disheartening was that, at the time, her daughter was but three. It starts so young!

In fact, the fear of rejection starts the moment we realize we are separate. The squeal of delight when our parents hid their faces playing peekaboo was only fun once we learned they were coming back. But, from before we can even remember, there were moments when they didn't return as fast as we wanted, through no fault of their own.

Oh, but we wanted as much attention and assurance as we could get. It's as if we intrinsically knew, even at the youngest ages, even before scientists studied human behavior, that more important than anything else was being close to people we loved. We knew every other need stemmed from having that one met.

Indeed, "Maslow had it wrong," social neuroscientist Dr. Matthew D. Lieberman says in his book *Social: Why Our Brains Are Wired to Connect*. "Food, water, and shelter are *not* the most basic needs for an infant." Rather, "our biology is built to thirst for connection *because* it is linked to our most basic survival needs." If we view humans from a basic evolutionary perspective, it's clear that people had to live in tribes—connected to each other—in order to survive.

Belonging to tribes is essential to humanity, however we're connected—whether by ethnicity or nationality; by our roles as daughters, sisters, wives, mothers; or where and how we choose to live. Tribes provide protection, resources, identity, and meaning.

You've perhaps heard about what's called the "Roseto Effect." In 1961 two doctors noted how the men of Roseto, Pennsylvania, enjoyed drastically lower instances of heart disease as compared to the national average. For the next fifty years they studied this Italian immigrant community, especially in comparison to the men of nearby towns, whose health outlooks matched that of the rest of the country.

The village people smoked and drank wine freely, and fried their sausages and meatballs in lard. The men participated in backbreaking and dangerous labor working in slate quarries two hundred feet below the ground; most of the women worked in blouse factories. By our standards today we'd be hard-pressed to say they were living "healthy" lives, and yet they seemed almost immune to one of the country's leading causes of death.

One of the sociologists studying Roseto, John G. Bruhn, wrote, "There was no suicide, no alcoholism, no drug addiction, and very little crime. They didn't have anyone on welfare. Then we looked at peptic ulcers. They didn't have any of those either. These people were dying of old age. That's it."

What they did find speaks to the benefits of having strong relationships. All Roseto homes contained at least three generations of family; the elderly were elevated to the "Supreme Court" instead of being placed "on the shelf"; meals were eaten with conversation and laughter; social clubs were robust; the entire community celebrated holidays and church festivals; women stopped and talked in the street; and men met at the pubs after work. In other words, their relationships sustained them, allowing them to live longer and, theoretically, happier lives than did most of the country.

Stephen Covey, author of *The 7 Habits of Highly Effective People*, concurs: "Next to physical survival, the greatest need of a human being is psychological survival—to be understood, to be affirmed, to be validated, to be appreciated." And in *Mind Over Medicine: Scientific Proof That You Can Heal Yourself*, Dr. Lissa Rankin wrote: "Intimacy is preventative medicine," insisting "copious scientific data proves that loneliness is a greater risk to your health than smoking or lack of exercise; and finding your tribe is better than any vitamin, diet, or exercise regimen."

Another author known for his research of healthy communities, Dan Buettner trekked around the world to see why some communities live so much longer than others. In his book *Blue Zones: Lessons for Living Longer from the People Who've Lived the Longest* he identified the nine healthiest traits that lead to longevity; among these, he concluded that being connected to others radically improves our health—whether that means living in social circles that support healthy behaviors, putting family first, or belonging to a church and regularly attending faith-based services. Basically, strong, positive relationships help us to live longer, healthier lives.

GENTLE TRUTH: We can't enjoy intimacy if we don't feel like we belong

That we are wired for connection means we hunger for acceptance. So it makes complete sense that to be rejected from our community, or to even think about being disconnected from those we love, would go against everything we know is good for us. And so it stands to reason that we will go to great costs to avoid rejection.

Rejection is undoubtedly a strong word.

For some of you, the very word lands dead center. You know the feeling of doubt after you send an email to someone you admire and don't hear back. You feel the anxiety when you walk into a party and, like a kid in the lunch room, not know whom to go talk with. You can feel the fear of looking stupid when put on the spot to recall information or answer a question in front of a group. You can feel unwanted if you've extended the last few invitations to someone who hasn't returned the favor. You live with the awareness of how much you want to impress people, be safe in a group, or be sure that you're okay with those around you.

For some of you, the idea of fearing rejection sounds foreign. Perhaps you view yourself as strong, confident, and self-assured. You shrug your shoulders when you don't get the job, flip anyone off if they hurt you, and wipe your hands clean of any drama. But I assure you, you, too—though perhaps manifesting it differently—want to feel good enough, to feel accepted.

In *The MindBody Code: How to Change the Beliefs That Limit Your Health, Longevity, and Success*, clinical neuropsychologist Dr. Mario Martinez says few things impact our immune system more than the wounds of shame, abandonment, and betrayal—which we might experience when we feel like we don't fit in, get ousted, or even choose to leave a tribe. Regardless of the details, we can readily suffer from "tribal shame," which can be devastating, paralyzing, and long-lasting.

A plea I hear frequently is "I just want to find my tribe," which implies that most of us don't feel connected *enough*. Research suggests there's only a 50 percent chance that our two closest friends know each other; as such, it's no surprise we don't feel we're woven safely into a net. So, even if no one is even rejecting us per se, we can still end up feeling like the little girl at the playground who didn't know who to play with.

And from a more spiritual perspective, Rabbi Harold Kushner wrote in *Conquering Fear: Living Boldly in an Uncertain World*: "The fear of rejection is perhaps the most shattering of all fears," one that impacts us more deeply than the fear of aging, terrorism, natural disasters, or death—because learning we are not valued cuts to our core, and often triggers our worst behavior. We'll cheat to win, we'll stalk to win back someone we've lost, we'll commit suicide after heartbreak, or we'll gun down those who let us go. Putting aside for a moment how most of us would never go to those extremes, wanting to belong is neither a weakness nor a condition shared by only those with low self-esteem; it's an essential of our humanity.

Even the "small" concerns can plague us. *("Did she really mean it when she said it was good to see me? Why didn't she email back?")* Everything from the individual level—the embarrassment of walking into a conference or a party alone, or the awkwardness of having under- or overdressed for an occasion—to everything that makes up our greater identities—our spouses, kids, and parents; our home, company, industry; our political party, religious community, even our hobbies—can be causes for concern. When our husbands say something embarrassing, we, too, feel the blush. When others attack the president we helped elect, we bristle as though personally rejected.

The Science of Feeling Excluded

For women, survival might be even more connected to our acceptance and integration with others. In *Playing Big: Find Your Voice, Your Mission, Your Message*, Tara Mohr wrote: "For most of history, likability and others' approval was women's lifeline." Without our own careers, property, voting rights, money, or superior physical strength, our survival was linked to our ability to comply with the rules set up by those with greater power, and our value came through which men begat us or married us. Getting that man to like us, and for the community to approve of us, was our best survival strategy.

We often describe it as, "I don't want to feel judged," or "I just never feel like I quite fit in," or "Everything is always about her," or "I'm tired of always trying to measure up." There are as many ways to nuance the feeling as there are different types of people, but at the core of all our fears is the ultimate fear of not being good enough to be accepted by those we admire and love.

In fact, that need for acceptance goes deeper than with just those in our immediate sphere: Research shows that we can be deeply stung from perceived ostracism even when it comes from people we don't like—or don't even know!

Dr. Kipling D. Williams, author of *Ostracism: The Power of Silence*, has described several studies he conducted that strangely defy rational thinking. One study at Purdue University showcased that even if a randomized computer game appears to leave us out, or favor someone else, the "seemingly trivial instances of ostracism provokes outsized emotional response." Our brain could remind us that it's impossible for a *computer* to reject or choose us, but it won't lessen the ache.

Another study he did at Leiden University in the Netherlands actually showed people feeling bad about being left out even if what they were being invited to would harm them! In other words, if being included in a game of catch meant that they lost money every time the ball was thrown to them, or that the ball was a bomb that could explode at any moment, participants still felt excluded if the ball wasn't thrown to them as often as it was to others.

In an article titled "The Pain of Exclusion," Dr. Williams wrote that the consequences of feeling excluded in any way registers in our brains as physical pain. He says in no uncertain terms that the emotional agony of perceived social isolation can activate "pain centers, incite sadness and anger, increase stress, lower self-esteem, and rob us of a sense of control."

Brain imaging scans demonstrate how feeling ignored triggers several parts of our brains, including the regions linked with physical agony. So much so that they discovered that analgesics (such as Tylenol or Advil) can actually reduce the feelings of "social separation just as they do physical pain." Or, in other words, our parents were wrong when they taught us that "Sticks and stones may break [our] bones, but words will never harm [us]."

How strange to consider that our neglect, silence, gossip, judgment, passive-aggressive remarks, cold shoulders, and name-calling can register as painfully real as would a punch to the gut or slap to the face. Such dismay casts a new light on the emotional bruises we have both given and received throughout our lives.

Worse, while bones and skin heal, the sting of not fitting in or of not being chosen becomes a lens through which we might view everything if we're not careful—or if we don't realize we're doing so. It's unfortunately easy to perceive everything in life as intended for or against us, to in fact take most things personally. From these tendencies we can develop patterns of only pushing back or slinking away—rather than taking another option: calmly standing our ground, assured of our value.

While the researchers note that this pain affects people of all personality types—confident and tough or depressed and fragile—with or without social anxiety, they also emphasize that character traits do affect how quickly we recover from life's psychological insults, and how much we let it cripple our future choices.

The fact that we want to belong isn't a result of brokenness in us, but is the result of the desire to love and care. That desire is beautiful. How we go about getting that need met, or how anxious we feel when it's not, might leave some room for growth, but the actual hunger is a pure, expansive, and inclusive aspiration.

It's human to want to belong.

I believe consistent practice of the exercises to follow can increase your resilience, bolster your self-esteem, and bond you to others in meaningful ways—so that when we're threatened with rejection, as we all will be, we can still feel connected and grounded, and can return to a place of feeling loved.

COURAGEOUS ACTIONS: Three Practices for Coping with Rejection

Since fear of rejection runs so deep, experiencing it can trigger the classic fight, flight, or freeze responses to stress. Which of the three that gets triggered most often derives from the established patterns of any one individual. When you feel rejected, what is your default mode: Do you lash out? Do you withdraw? Do you cling?

Studies show that, whatever train we tend to jump on, we bring with us baggage of hostility and defensiveness. So if we are prone to pull away and hide when we feel shunned, then often we also soothe ourselves by devaluing the other person. (*"She's such a narcissist—I'm better off without her anyway."*) If we're likely to attack, then we might respond with verbal or physical abuse. But regardless of how we react, it unfortunately appears that nearly all of us, if given the opportunity, feel instinctively compelled to act out against those who exclude us.

But that doesn't mean that's how we want to live our lives. There is a vast difference between instinctive reactions and intuitive responses. And while the first may feel easier, the latter is where maturity resides. So, if our goal is to react less and respond more, then we need to identify which situations tend to threaten us. Once we've articulated when we're susceptible, we can work to catch ourselves in the act—so we can instead choose compassion and tenderness. And then we want to do it again the next time we're triggered—and then again, until ultimately we've created new neural pathways with healthy rather than destructive responses. We cannot forge intimacy with pity or hatred, whether toward ourselves or others.

Now, this is not a simple task, for two reasons. The muscle memory of our established pathways is so strong we can readily, unconsciously, slip into our old ruts as if they were our only option. As Harvard psychiatrist Dr. Srinivasan S. Pillay described in *Life Unlocked: 7 Revolutionary Lessons to Overcome Fear*, to relearn responses we have to commit to two processes: extinction and imprinting. With extinction we remove the learned response; with imprinting we learn new responses—establishing new pathways through the nerve centers in the brain.

The other reason? We often consciously resist just this sort of growth because it's hard work, and because we have to give up whatever reward we associate with our established response, be that the pride of believing we're right or the comforting familiarity of licking our wounds. But those old autopilot "friends" aren't leading us to greater frientimacy, so we'll want to heal a few leaks by forging new roads. Here are three practices that have worked for me.

Practice #1: Retrain Your Brain to Assume Acceptance

First, we'll want to identify *situations* that trigger our feeling rejected in some way, such as:

- We don't hear back from others as quickly as we'd like—or at all!

- We see photos on Facebook of our friends having fun with *other* friends.

- We walk into a crowded party where we know no one.

- The people we're talking to don't affirm us. Or we tell a story that gets no reaction whatsoever.

- Someone challenges our decisions.

Note that, while it's important to identify what our triggers are so we can work on them, we also want to learn to be extra gentle and loving with ourselves in those hurtful moments.

Second, we'll want to look at exactly *how* these scenarios make us feel—not just "rejected," but also its variety of cousins. For example, can you imagine any of the above situations leaving you feeling:

- Ashamed?

- Boring or stupid?

- Dismissed?

- Excluded?

- Ignored?

- Invisible?

- Second-string? Third-wheel?

- Slighted?

- Unimportant?

In my experience, most of the time when we feel bad it's because we *assume* that the other person's actions indicate we aren't valued. So let's stop and recognize that probably 99 percent of the time the "rejecting" person didn't flat out say: "I reject you. Go away." This isn't to say that never happens; it is to say it's incredibly easy to slip into the "I'm being rejected" rut in situations where nothing of the kind is at play.

So, if upon scrutiny we realize we've been making negative assumptions in those situations, why not practice defaulting to positive assumptions instead? Let's instead keep our hearts open, practicing giving our friends the benefit of the doubt. Let's assume, unless they distinctly tell us otherwise, that our friends accept us, like us, and love us—and proceed from there.

When we recognize in the moment that we feel left out or shunned, what if, instead of fighting, fleeing, or freezing, we went through a mental process something like this:

1. *Compassion*: I need to be gentle with myself right now. What is the most loving thing I can do to bring myself back to a place where I feel my value?

2. *Reiterate self-worth*: Some part of me knows that my value is stable, independent of any interaction or circumstance. So I choose to trust that, even if I *feel* less-than, I know I am just as loveable, pure, and good as ever.

3. *Check-in*: From a place of knowing I'm still valuable, I want to acknowledge that, while I don't like how my friend treated me, she is of course valuable, too. I'm going to assume that what she did/said has little to do with me and more to do with her. If I'm willing to reserve judgment, what do I *really* know about this situation? Was her slight done unintentionally—was she just unaware? What are all the different things she *could* have meant? Or is she hurting in some way? Did it maybe "start" with me: Did I say or do something that made her feel threatened? Most likely we're two people doing the best we can.

4. *Make a decision*: Is there anything I can do right now to increase the chances of both of us walking away feeling loved? What if I ask her to explain what she meant? Should I better communicate my feelings or needs? What if I were to follow up, giving her another chance to stay connected? What, if anything, can I do to amplify love to myself and her?

To provide an example, let's take a real-life scenario from one of the women in one of my CoachingCircles. On an earlier visit to her mother, Stephanie had texted a friend who lived nearby to see if she had time to meet up for dinner. Crickets, she never heard back. This made her feel discounted. She also acknowledged that she and her friend had drifted apart somewhat, since they didn't talk frequently or live locally. Understandably, she felt insecure and uncertain about the friendship. But when she again visited her mother, though the old her would have remained sore and not contacted her friend, this time, even though she felt nervous about it, she reached out again—and this time she gave her more advance notice and both emailed *and* texted her. What happened? The two friends closed down the restaurant, talking long into the evening.

FOR REFLECTION: See the "Charting Situations that Trigger" exercise on the next page.

FOR PRACTICE: Like the woman who reached out to her friend again when she was visiting her mother, consider a time when you didn't do something for fear of rejection. Instead of assuming rejection, can you practice assuming acceptance and reach out again?

Charting Situations That Trigger Feelings of Rejection

Start an ongoing chart to track different situations where you can end up feeling rejected in some way. In the first column, list all the situations you can think of that leave you feeling slighted. In the second column, note how these situations make you feel. In the third column, write in how you tend to react in those situations.

Situations	Feelings	Reactions	Explanations	Alternatives
What triggered feelings of rejection?	How did the situation make you feel?	How did you react? Or how do you tend to react?	What are some explanations for the situation that don't have to do with you?	Assuming the best instead of the worst, what could you do instead?
Texted old friend to say would be in town, can we get together. Friend never replied.	Discounted. Insecure and uncertain about the friendship.	Feeling hurt, was inclined to not contact her again the next time I was in town.	Maybe she never got the text; maybe she was overwhelmed with life at the time.	Contact her again, this time by email and text, and see what happens. If she doesn't reply, I'll send her a follow-up email to say "hope we can get together next time."

Now, for the fourth column, explanations for the situation that don't have to do with you, the pessimists in your life or in your head might ask: "But what if it did have to do with you? What if the friend was trying to ignore you or get rid of you?"

Most of us often assume the worst—and are wrong much of the time. Maybe it's time we assume the best by default, and risk being wrong a few times. What would be the worst case scenario? We'd force our friend's hand, making her express her feelings more directly, which would either give us the opportunity to really talk about it, or would simply confirm what we feared and would have believed anyway. Just a little more effort leaves us either where we'd have been anyway—but clear about that fact—or, more likely, has deepened the intimacy in that friendship. So complete the final column: assuming the best instead of the worst, what could you do instead?

My philosophy is that if people want to reject me, then they need to be super clear about it. Otherwise, I've trained myself to assume nothing's amiss unless I hear otherwise. And though retraining the brain like this won't be easy, if this path invites me to live life with less fear of rejection, then it's well worth the effort.

We experience another form of rejection when we feel judged. Consider the following scenarios:

- We're given advice when all we really wanted was validation.
- We sense the passive-aggressive statements tossed into conversation.
- We feel we're pushed to do something we're not ready to act on.
- We feel the angst of making decisions we know someone doesn't agree with.
- We hold shame that our lives don't look the way others, or we, expect them to.
- We hear others' condemnation for our behavior, appearance, or choices.
- We feel ignored after we shared something that really matters to us.

When we perceive we're being judged we can feel attacked, blamed, or accused. I know I've often felt some of these responses:

- We might convince ourselves any negative remarks are unfounded.
- We might fear others will agree with accusations against us.
- We might want others to understand us and our motives.
- We might fear being controlled or pushed around.
- We might feel the need to defend our choices.
- We might feel the need to be right and blameless.

I'd guess that, more often than not, when we feel defensive the other wasn't even trying to offend. But, no matter: when we're the ones in the boxing ring, sometimes it's not a hug we want, but rather a referee who holds up our hand in victory for all to see.

I strongly relate to this need. I like to be right, feel understood, and have others admire me. So when attacked, I defend—not with temper-tantrums, tears, or insults necessarily, just with calm, mature rationalizing. At least that's what I used to tell myself! I really believed for much of my life that being defensive was like being on moral high ground, like an act of self-righteousness—the way a kid tries to get out of trouble by saying "I didn't start it."

Then I read Dr. Helen Schucman's *A Course in Miracles* and gulped when I read, "To defend is to attack." What?!?!

Of course, my first reaction was to feel defensive, seeking evidence to support my right to defend. Ha! But something in me switched that day, as I began to believe that my defensive language was no more honorable than being the verbal attacker. My behavior didn't change easily or immediately, but I began to watch how I, and those around me, did indeed either create or escalate angst with defensiveness. By our very defending, we were the ones energizing the fight. One person saying something doesn't make a fight; it's the second one to respond that says, "Game on!" In defending myself I was creating a stronger sense of rejection, widening the gap between me and the other.

And I compared that behavior to that of "grace-walkers," as I like to call them, who seem to live in peace no matter the circumstances. They laugh at themselves instead of taking everything so seriously; they ask questions to learn more instead of taking on the need to explain; and they either apologize quickly or let the "assault" roll off their backs. They weren't caught up in fights, they weren't tense, and they didn't look like they felt diminished in any way.

So, what to do? We'd all be wise to practice not focusing on defending ourselves but instead on *being* ourselves—and on letting go of the need to win everyone over, to be understood all the time. It started for me by just saying "This time I'm going to experiment with not taking this personally."

Friendspiration: "I'm going to experiment with
not taking everything personally."

Another option would be to practice nondefensiveness by simply asking for what we need. What if we said to our advice-giving friends, "Oh thank you for your advice, but actually what I need right now isn't someone trying to solve my problem, but just someone to listen and empathize with me."

Every time I've tried that, I have received what I asked for, which increased the bond and eliminated the need for me to defend.

Defensiveness Can Hurt Us More Than It Hurts Others

Every time we defend against something real or perceived, we stress our bodies and brains, using our energy to survive instead of to digest, relax, and heal. Thanks to extensive research by brain experts and psychologists, we know that our immediate physiological response to assault is to release into our systems the stress hormones cortisol and norepinephrine. This release leads to a faster heartbeat, quicker breathing, higher blood pressure, expanded blood vessels, activated muscles, dilated pupils, and eventually exhaustion and depression. Not only are these responses draining, they also sabotage opportunities for making the connections we most crave. How?

Dr. Srinivasan Pillay, who teaches how the brain receives signals and processes fear, emphasizes that this almost instinctive fear response is the greatest obstacle to trust—which is essential for us to feel attached to others. He says: "If you look for something through the lens of fear, your brain will pick up only fear-related things. If you look for something through a lens of hope, you will pick up hopeful things." (Indeed, such is the premise behind practicing gratitude.)

What we're learning from neuroscience gets even more life-enriching, even exciting. Our brains are way more moldable and changeable (referred to as neuroplasticity) than we've previously acknowledged. In fact, we can essentially create new neural pathways in our brains. How? By unplugging our default thoughts and practicing new ones. Much the way paths are made through forests or fields—the more we walk a new route, the more cleared it becomes, and the less we walk the other route, the more overgrown it becomes. This, my friends, is how we can learn to walk with grace instead of with a stick.

I'm also learning that there really are few situations where it's worth jumping in. So I invite you to walk with greater grace, and to respond to perceived or actual affronts with an open heart rather than a closed fist.

FOR REFLECTION: Consider a recent incident when you defended yourself against a perceived affront. Can you remember how you felt at the time? What you did at the time? Can you replay the scene in your mind, responding in a manner that doesn't take it too personally?

FOR PRACTICE: Do you often feel judged by a particular friend? Perhaps because she gives unrequested advice or makes jokes that sting? Practice saying to her, "While I appreciate your advice, what I actually need is . . ." or sharing, "You know, that joke stings a bit. It makes me feel . . ." Then, decide to lovingly practice the next time you feel tempted to defend.

Practice #3: Retrain Your Brain to Trust Others

In the "Defensiveness" sidebar above I noted that neuroscientist Dr. Srinivasan Pillay cites how we cannot feel attached to others if we feel we cannot trust them. This fact can be problematic for those who would say: "But what do I do if I have trust issues? People have disappointed me . . . so I'm scared to let them get too close."

For those who would ask that question there's a decision to be made: Do you want to be someone who always has trust issues, or do you want to, someday, be someone who trusts people? But be clear—your trust issues are *your* issue, not a reflection of the people you're meeting.

Some of us can work through our stuff on our own, and some of us might find it too hard to go it alone. There's no blame or shame in seeking therapy. Indeed, sometimes therapy is essential for teaching us how to let go of the pain we feel—and perhaps also forgive those who have hurt us. In therapy we can learn how to establish and maintain boundaries, and practice letting people in incrementally. Remember, the Frientimacy Triangle has us increase the risk only incrementally, in alignment with the consistency, so we're never taking a huge risk, throwing our big trust on someone who hasn't proven trustworthy in the small matters. But, at the end of the day, love is indeed a risk. And it's a risk we have to take if we want greater intimacy in our lives.

Dr. Brené Brown, who has researched shame for decades, has shown that if we shy away from vulnerability—thinking that it protects us from shame—that we are, indeed, shying away from the core of our feelings, including many of the "good" feelings we want to feel. In her book *Daring Greatly: How the Courage to Be Vulnerable Transforms the Way We Live, Love, Parent, and Lead*, she wrote: "To believe vulnerability is weakness is to believe that feeling is weakness. To foreclose on our emotional life out of a fear that the costs will be too high is to walk away from the very thing that gives purpose and meaning to living."

Therefore it's not just potential rejection that we're blocking when we buttress our walls with extra protection—it's also possible acceptance. Because to shut off feeling negative emotions we have to also close the valve on the positive ones; we can't pick and choose. If we want love, we must risk heartache. Meaningful connection is what can heal the heart. It is what mends disappointment, betrayal, and rejection.

Friendspiration: "I will take more incremental risks because I want greater intimacy in my life."

Some women say the best part of maturity is caring less what everyone else thinks. I for one have no desire to wait for that peace—I will do all I can *right now* to hear my inner wisdom over the voice of my fear.

To some it feels like a conundrum: "*I have to risk rejection in order to feel acceptance.*" However, remember that another's rejection of us has *nothing* to do with our worth. We are still the same person, with the same gifts, the same smile, the same passion, and the same value today as yesterday. Know that we are safe—even when we feel rejected. We are still lovable, still worthy, still powerful, still capable, still good—even when we feel rejected.

Much of the risk of rejection is an illusion. Tender self-care, increased self-awareness, and practice at loving ourselves can help us to see that rejection isn't the scary beast we've been losing sleep over. Rejection is more like the Wizard of Oz: something that looks so big, so omniscient and omnipotent—but which is really just a man with a few tricks hiding behind a curtain.

The answer isn't in bolstering our walls; it's in bolstering our heart with love. It isn't in keeping people at a safe distance; it's letting enough love in to help us ride the inevitable disappointments. The way through isn't in hiding from everyone; it's in revealing our worth: to ourselves and to others.

Yes, the fear feels real; yes, it's unnerving to move closer to the shadow; yes, it's sad to think of someone not loving us in the ways we want. But when we decide we crave meaningful connection more than we fear heartache— and then decide to embrace life rather than hide from it—we will be well on our way to building the bridge that spans our intimacy gap.

FOR REFLECTION: Consider whether you have limited intimacy with one or more of your friends on account of having trust issues. Can you imagine trusting that person a bit more? What would that look like? Can you imagine what might be the worst that would happen if you did—and can you survive that?

FOR PRACTICE: Select a friend you will work to open yourself to more. Think of how you might go about it—and plan to do it.

We Are Good and Safe

If you feel defensive reading this, like I'm asking for the impossible, I totally understand. And it may be that I am a bit idealistic.

If having been grossly mistreated in your past has left you with little trust and lots of fear, if you've been given little reason to have faith in others, then the vision I'm casting could seem grandiose—certainly more than it would feel to those who bond with relative security. Either way this is a big ask. It's like inviting someone to train for a marathon. But growth isn't all or nothing—it's not a choice between running a marathon or cheering from the sidelines. We can choose to walk a 5K, or even just a 1K, and still be healthier than if we had done nothing.

Think of my goddaughter Lily, who at just three years old and in preschool was already feeling the sting of being left out. What would you tell her? Would you hope that she'd grow up loving herself and trusting others? Or would you project your own fears on her, advising her to trust no one and to play alone? Most of us will find it easier to be more compassionate with her than we would with ourselves. I mean, we feel justified in *our* defensiveness because we know what we've had to do to survive. But if we picture her, and see her purity, her innocence, and her beauty, then can we not give to ourselves that same sense of hope for a better path forward? Can we not wish for her a lifetime of feeling so loved that she welcomes it where it's offered—and never feels diminished when it doesn't always come? If so, what wisdom would you say to her? Can you not gift yourself with that same wisdom?

In *Scary Close*, Donald Miller wrote: "There are more lifeguards than sharks." Very few people out there actually want to reject us. In most cases, what we encounter is just a beach full of people, like ourselves, trying to swim the best they can, just like we do. We can trust that the waters are far friendlier than we fear.

Read on to learn more about the power to be found in trusting others!

Worth Remembering

- The second fear that stands in the way of frientimacy is the fear of rejection. This fear is so strong because we are hardwired to want to belong.

- We can train ourselves to choose healthier responses to moments when we feel rejected. We can respond with compassion, we can reiterate our self-worth, we can check in with the person who hurt us, and we can decide to respond with love instead of by lashing out or withdrawing.

- We can practice not focusing on defending ourselves but instead on *being* ourselves—and choosing to not take things too personally. We can also practice nondefensiveness by simply asking for what we need.

- If we want love, we must risk heartache—and that means allowing ourselves to trust others. Meaningful connection is what can heal the heart. It is what mends disappointment, betrayal, and rejection.

Next up: how jumping to toxic conclusions about each other limits our frientimacy.

11

Obstacle to Intimacy #3: The Toxic Friend Trend

Or, The Fear *They* Aren't Good Enough

It seems like everyone I'm meeting these days is either a sociopath or narcissist." While hopefully this comment, voiced by someone in the audience at one of my talks, is more extreme than most of us would admit to, it does showcase a concern I've heard repeatedly: "I can't find anyone who's as healthy and self-aware as I am." Indeed, in a friendship study of 18,000 women and 4,000 men, 84 percent of women responding revealed they'd had a toxic friend, one-third of which were the respondents' best friends.

We're often told that the healthiest or most mature among us actively eliminate all imperfect (read: toxic) people from our lives, biding by such mantras as:

- "People inspire you, or they drain you. Pick wisely."
- "If their presence can't add value to your life, then their absence will make no difference."
- "Surround yourself with only people who are going to lift you higher."

The above sayings and others have emerged from books and articles giving "permission," primarily to women, to stop putting up with the unhealthy people in our lives, people who have been dubbed such names as the Copycat, the Doormat, the Leech, the Misery Lover, and the User.

Headlines like "Ten Signs Your Friend Is Toxic" and "How to Recognize a Toxic Friend" tout the skills of weeding out these wolves in sheep's clothing. With some advice I've seen, the diplomacy of the statements in the previous bullet list are replaced with much more fraught commands:

- "Kick her to the curb!"
- "Dump her!"
- "Detox from her."
- "Upgrade your friends."
- "End it now!"

If we were to follow this popular advice, we'd remain on high alert, always on the lookout for the next potential culprit to avoid. But that method would have us approach friendships the way a detective seeks clues at a crime scene. The only problem is that no crime has happened, and the chances of a friendship blossoming out of skepticism and doubt drops exponentially as people feel auditioned and judged, prodded and evaluated.

No wonder we're lonely: We're scared of letting imperfect people get too close to us. And far too easily we buy in to the theory that we "just" need to find the *right* people: the few in this world who would not only get us, love us, and accept us—but also be worthy of us. These "needle in a haystack" odds leave us with few choices: Dismiss most people as inadequate and search elsewhere; convince ourselves it's a lost cause and resign to feeling disconnected, but safe; or put up with the friends we have even though they're not what we want. Of course, none of this leads us to the intimacy we crave.

The word "toxic" comes from the Latin word *toxicum*, a "poisoned arrow." From that origin derived the clinical definition of toxic, which is used to describe personality disorders and psychoses inclined to inflict harm on the self and others. The gravity of these definitions belie how the popular media attribute as "toxic" behaviors that, in truth, *all* of us exhibit from time to time: being critical, flakey, jealous, pessimistic, or self-obsessed. It's so easy to decide that *they* "out there" are the toxic ones, from whom we must defend ourselves, but in truth it's not that simple.

I believe the gross misuse of the word "toxic" has greatly damaged both our relationships and our sense of self. It's bad enough that the news convinces us that we can't trust the people on the other side of the world, those who vote for the other candidate, or those who walk into our schools. To extend that to say we can't rely on our friends anymore creates an anxiety that leaves very few of us feeling safe. This is unacceptable to me. First, let's reserve the term "toxic" for those who undeniably point their arrows with malicious intent. Then, for the less malicious we'd otherwise dub toxic, let's instead simply recognize that they are, in fact, works in progress—as we all are.

Emotional health—a broad umbrella that can include such things as emotional intelligence, self-actualization, and spiritual growth—is a scale, a continuum, not a yes-or-no answer. As an illustration, the founders of the *Emotional Intelligence 2.0* inventory rate, on a scale between 0 and 100 percent, use four categories to measure Emotional Intelligence (EQ): self-awareness, self-management, social awareness, and relationship management. Most of us fall in the middle.

But far more important than just realizing we aren't only all good or all bad is recognizing that our scores also frequently change, fluctuating in response to the various circumstances we encounter in life. In their book *The Wisdom of the Enneagram: The Complete Guide to Psychological and Spiritual Growth for the Nine Personality Types*, which uses a 1–9 scale to identify whether we act from our healthiest or unhealthiest selves, authors

Don Riso and Russ Hudson remind us that, while we may each default to one number, our range in any given day can move up or down by two numbers. That means someone who scores a 5 can behave anywhere between 3 and 7, depending on her stress levels and responses. As such, we can see how easily we might observe a friend sometimes seeming healthy and other times not. It doesn't mean we're now seeing her "real character." Her level-7 behaviors are no more real than her level-3 behaviors—they are all her. She's just living in her range, appearing healthier when she's engaged in self-care and surrounded by support, and exhibiting unhealthy behaviors when she's scared and tired. It's important to keep this in mind: For every friend we'd be inclined to discount for any one-time assessment, the same assessment could be equally made of *us* at another time.

For example, which of the following have you on occasion been guilty of?

- Being self-obsessed in general
- Being short when we need to get off the phone
- Canceling on a date
- Commandeering the conversation absent-mindedly
- Forgetting birthdays and other milestones
- Interrupting when someone is speaking
- One-upping a story with one of our own
- Saying something easily taken the wrong way
- Sounding critical

It is a given that throughout our relationships we all, even the healthiest among us, will fail to meet expectations—repeatedly. So let's freely acknowledge that we don't always present to our friends the most enlightened, healthy, and happy versions of ourselves, nor do they. So, when others fail us at times, which of course they will, the trick is not to judge, dismiss, and continue searching; the trick is to judge less, observe more, and continue working on ourselves. Rather than assuming others aren't worthy of us until they've earned our trust, let's proceed from an understanding, much like our court system, that everyone is innocent of friendship wrongdoing unless found to be guilty.

We Can Acknowledge Imperfection and Strive to Improve

Our goal is to create friendships that allow for imperfect actions—theirs and ours—without letting those actions threaten the friendship. My best friendships are the ones where I *know* I can cancel last minute and she won't take it personally, where if I forget her birthday she won't for a second think I don't love her, and where I can go on and on about something one evening and not wake up the next morning with a hangover of regret and self-recrimination.

The question isn't whether we should let needy or depressed people into our lives—we do, and we should. Rather, the question is *how much* we let them in, and for what purpose. Our closest friends are those with whom we incrementally move up the Frientimacy Triangle—practicing positivity, consistency, and vulnerability as regularly as possible. Most likely not everyone can climb to the top with you, but that doesn't mean those "less-fulfilled" friendships don't deserve to share the Triangle with you.

The truth is that we have to learn to be around people who can hurt—those prone to judge, whine, attack, and defend. We're related to some of them, we work for some of them, and sometimes we have been—or still are—those people ourselves. But this isn't a world made up of friends and enemies; rather, it's a world of friends and people to be friendly toward. Hurting, jealous, still-growing, unhealthy people are not our enemies—they are people with a lot of work ahead of them who deserve our compassion, not our rancor. And while we don't have to foster friendships with people we consider to be unhealthy, we do have to figure out how to keep being kind.

Just To Be Clear

I am not advocating any relationship that lacks the clear boundaries necessary to maintain your emotional and physical safety. What I *am* saying is that most of us are so scared of mistakes, flaws, weaknesses, and deficiency that we are limiting ourselves to a bunch of shallow relationships—for if we go any deeper we will always find that our friends aren't perfect. Ironically, finding those imperfections, and not being phased by them, is actually the hallmark of any deep connection.

It's not our perfect façades that keep us knit together, but our willingness to expose the truth that we're all still on the journey.

If your own light is dim or flickering, then perhaps you may need to set some boundaries and limit time with people you feel can't support the happier and more powerful version of yourself. But know, too, that that's temporary, and something to own in yourself rather than to blame in others.

COURAGEOUS ACTIONS: Five Practices for Owning Up

It so happens that in practicing being kind—especially with those we'd previously want to shun—*we* will grow in the process. We will build stronger muscles as we engage in our compassion, provoke our empathy, and develop our ability to set boundaries.

When we show up differently, it changes the pattern and the dynamic of the relationship—and in turn invites the other to respond differently. Chances are high that our friend won't respond perfectly the first time we practice, nor will we initiate perfectly. That's why we call it *practice*. And know that the point is not to reach immediate success. If we feel it's important to stay in relationship with this person, the point is we're choosing to become people more likely to hold our peace through whatever comes—and to in turn be an agent of peace.

To follow are five practices that can help us to own up.

Our temptation is to always see the fault in the other. But given that the study cited earlier noted 84 percent of women claim to have had a toxic friend, then that can mean only one of two things: 1) that we've all been friends with the same 16 percent of the population who is toxic; or 2) that, to someone else, *we* are the toxic one.

One of the more poignant quotes from *The Wisdom of the Enneagram* references our inability to accurately gauge our own level of health: "we tend to see *our* motivations as coming from the healthy range. The defenses of our ego are such that we always see ourselves as our idealized self-image, *even when we are only average or even pathological.*"

In other words, we all have some crazy in us! We all have shadows of unhealthy: insecurities, wounds, fears, and jealousies. We all have habits that are hard to break, and we all can get distracted, obsessed, distant, and intense. We all bump into each other as we chug along in our hectic lives. So let's start this practice from a place of humility, acknowledging up front what we bring to each relationship.

Friendspiration: "I want to keep growing and learning."

The more I study and value myself, the more my defense mechanisms drop, and the more I'm able to see my own motivations, triggers, and tendencies. Much like those who'd say: "The more I study this subject, the more I realize how little I know," we will know we're maturing when we aren't as convinced that everyone around us needs to change. Like teenagers who think they know the most, we're being called to grow up.

FOR REFLECTION: Take the Enneagram test online (www.enneagraminstitute.com/guide-to-all-riso-hudson-tests#TESTS). Once you've identified your type, study its description. Work to read it from a place of nondefensiveness, neither denying your shadows nor your tendencies. Then consider how, according to this assessment, your motives and default responses might be impacting your friendships. Can you imagine how you might work to shift those responses?

FOR PRACTICE: Starting today, when you engage with people, try to observe yourself in action to see if you can catch yourself reacting in responses you've identified as unhealthy. (For example, see how I practiced changing behavior on page 19.) For now, just observe it. Eventually, you'll experiment with reacting differently.

Practice #2: Assume the Best in Others

In a world where we can screen calls, ignore emails, bully in blog comments, and "unfriend" with a click, we are at ever greater risk of seeing each other as objects, things we can just as easily discard as retain.

One way we do this is by labeling people—as Doormat, Leech, User, etc. But since humans are far too complex to be shoved into one simple category, any label we assign will be both incorrect and unhelpful.

We also fail ourselves by choosing those toxic labels precipitously—and then reversing them when things go sour. For example, when someone disappoints us—whether we know them or not—some of us are prone to believe we *now* see that person's "true" nature, as though everything else were a mirage. Whether he's your elected politician or your next-door neighbor, if he makes a mistake we'll decide his authentic self—be it swindling or conniving or philandering—has finally emerged. But as much as we speak of a wolf in sheep's clothing, we rarely reverse the concept. Have you ever noted "Now, I see his *true* nature" when someone we dislike behaves in a kind or respectable way? Well, why not?

Friendspiration: "I am willing to see the good in people."

Far too often we believe that the mistakes and imperfections of others are more their "real" selves than all the good they also are. And the real trouble is that assuming the worst in others can be more fatal to friendships than the initial perceived mistake. If we are committed to forging deeper connections, we have to practice looking for and believing in the best in others.

FOR REFLECTION: Are there people you've thought of or described as toxic? If so, specify in what way they're toxic. Are they greedy? Narcissistic? Flakey? Needy? Our brains have a habit of finding evidence to support our opinions, but that doesn't mean there isn't also evidence that could support a more complete—or even completely different—picture. Take a moment to focus solely on their positive traits. Have they beauty and goodness? Bouts of generosity? This isn't to say those positive traits negate, erase, or excuse their flaws; this is to say we want to be people who practice seeing *all* of people, not just the parts we're particularly frustrated by. Try to list as many good qualities as you can, including times they loved you well and occasions where they responded outside what will hopefully become their *former* label.

FOR PRACTICE: Note that those you've negatively labeled have most likely intuitively picked up on your judgment. So, today make an effort to actively look for and verbally affirm their positive attributes. Perhaps say, "That was thoughtful of you," or "I always love how you do that." That's it. And watch in the future for ways you could repeat the practice.

Practice #3: Work to Understand Others' Needs

> "She always complains. Nothing is good enough for her. No matter how much good I point out to her, she focuses on the negative."

> "She's never satisfied. She's obsessed with making more money, becoming more beautiful, achieving more. I told her she just needs to be content with what she has, or she'll never be happy!"

We likely all know someone we consider a "complainer": the person who talks endlessly about the same problem, or who leaves one problem just to seek out another, and then talks endlessly about that. Of course talking through our problems with each other is what friends do, but we can get understandably weary of offering the same friendly, supportive, caring advice to the friend just to have her come back for another large helping next week.

Sometimes, exhausted at the thought of offering yet another pep talk, we can be inclined to ignore or push away that friend rather than feed what we might fear is an insatiable need. But it so happens that that instinctive approach can be more problematic than effective. That's because many of the behaviors that annoy us in others derive from a sense of shame and fear, so our fear of her need only adds fuel to the causes of her behavior.

Researcher Dr. David R. Hawkins describes in *Power vs. Force: The Hidden Determinants of Human Behavior* how shame and fear, two of the weakest thought patterns we engage in, drain our energy and discourage our initiative. So, if we ignore or diminish a pessimistic friend, her shame and fear will likely increase, our intimacy will reduce, our objective will have backfired, and we'll have offered pain instead of love to our friendship. Is that who we want to be?

People are more likely to change when they feel strong and safe and loved. So what if, instead of trying to distract our negative friend with positive thoughts, we experiment with empathizing with her, like by saying, "Oh that does sound so stressful!" Much like a child with a scraped knee comes crying to Mom for comfort first and Band-Aid second, when we experience a pain of some kind, we need to acknowledge it and grieve it before we can move on from it.

Friendspiration: "I believe in the power of love
and compassion to transform."

The same applies to our grown friends. The best first thing we can offer is not support and advice, but validation and acknowledgment. This might look like: "I'm so sorry you feel that every man you meet is noncommittal; that must be so discouraging." Or: "It makes sense that you feel you'll never find someone to love, given what a rough time of it you've had." In fact, it might be best to not offer advice at all, but instead to ask the friend what is the best thing you could do to help her right then. Maybe she'll request advice, but then again, maybe she just really needs an ear and a hug and a reminder that she is loved and loveable.

FOR REFLECTION: Choose a friend to view through a lens of compassion. Assuming for a moment that her behavior comes from a place of shame or fear, does any wisdom come to you about what might be driving her behavior? Can you imagine what pain might lead to this habit? (Of course, you don't know without asking, and she may not know, so simply consider it.)

FOR PRACTICE: Can you think of one behavior you could do the next time you see your friend that might help validate her feelings? (This doesn't mean you have to agree with her feelings—simply to acknowledge their existence, to acknowledge to your friend that she feels them.) Compassion, tenderness, curiosity, or affirmation might diffuse her shame, give her the space to process her fears, or help her feel seen—and ultimately more strong. Consider offering her this gift.

Practice #4: Rethink the Word "Needy"

Let us not forget that we all have needs. Being "needy" doesn't indicate a flaw of character, but an expression of the quest for connection. We need each other and we need to feel connected—and we do so with a hunger that is both healthy and human.

Ongoing studies have been examining what is called the "dependency paradox," which has demonstrated that the more dependent we are on each other the more independent and creative we are. In unpacking this theory, psychiatrist and neuroscientist Dr. Amir Levine and his coauthor Rachel

Heller note in their book *Attached: The New Science of Adult Attachment and How It Can Help You Find—and Keep—Love* how "attachment principles teach us that most men and women are only as needy as their unmet needs. When their emotional needs are met, they usually turn their attention outward."

Multiple studies have found that in romantic relationships our partners impact and regulate our blood pressure, our heart rates, our breathing rates, and even the levels of hormones in our blood. "Dependence is a fact; it is not a choice or preference." Friendships and other platonic relationships obviously won't impact us as strongly, but to recognize that we all need each other and are intrinsically intertwined is not something to feel shame over. It's important to keep that in mind the next time we're told that too much dependence in relationships is something to be avoided.

To be sure, some people struggle to bond and attach in fulfilling ways, and can showcase their insecurities by clinging or avoiding. But it's important to acknowledge that the problem isn't in having the need, but in how some people go about *meeting* that need. It is ultimately every individual's work to learn the skills of communicating feelings and practicing trust and security in relationships. But that doesn't mean we can't be in relationship with those who are "needy"; indeed, we can facilitate their growth by contributing to their sense of trust.

Friendspiration: "Needs are meant to be met with love."

Even if we tend to feel secure and confident in our relationships, thereby exhibiting less anxiety in our interactions, most of us will admit we want to know there are people we can depend on. That's part of what makes us feel safe, part of why we're drawn to closing our intimacy gaps. Since *we* want to have those who will be there for us, no matter what, that means in turn we should choose—when we can—to be that person for others.

FOR REFLECTION: Think of someone who feels needy to you. What is it you feel she's asking for? Or even hungering for? Can you identify what feelings that triggers in you: incompetence? Exhaustion? Guilt? A sense of responsibility? Can you imagine a scenario where her asks, demands, insatiability, or neediness didn't feel negative? Can you imagine situations where you could give what she needs and could say "no" if you couldn't?

FOR PRACTICE: Based on your answer to the above, how might you experiment with changing the dynamic between you and that person so your peace doesn't get uprooted by her needs? Are there better boundaries you can set between you? Is there perhaps an honest conversation you could initiate? A certain narrative or belief that needs updating? What actions can you take to practice shifting this relationship?

Practice #5: Trust That You Are Safe

The following email illustrates how quickly this fear of believing in the good in people can damage any hope of intimacy:

> "I feel like giving up on my goals of adding connection because I realize that two of my friends are passive-aggressive and basically selfish. I feel a little sick inside because I am afraid that everyone might be like that. They were the only people I was somewhat close to so I'm back to zero. I'm still giving them the appearance of being friends but I'm planning on distancing myself. I'm starting to lose hope in making any meaningful connections. I want to withdraw and protect myself from being treated badly. I am losing trust in people."

She undoubtedly hoped that I would assure her that she's wise to walk away from people she has determined are "passive-aggressive and basically selfish," but she showcases in her very dilemma where that choice leads to: loneliness, loss of hope, self-protection, and broken trust in humanity.

And remember, we're not talking about abuse here. We're talking about a pattern of noting a few problematic behaviors, diagnosing someone as "unfit," and then justifying withdrawal from the friendship. In essence, the pattern is *repeatedly* doing an about-face and fleeing before looking a friend in the face and really seeing.

Giving up and pulling away, or simply "giving them the appearance of being friends," guarantees that we never reach the connection we crave. While it might feel safe, it's not fulfilling—and we're the ones who lose out.

C. S. Lewis says it beautifully: "To love at all is to be vulnerable. Love anything and your heart will be wrung and possibly broken. If you want to make sure of keeping it intact you must give it to no one." If we withdraw, we remain isolated. But if we lean in with vulnerability, though at times we may get hurt, we will also at times connect and experience love. That really is the only way forward. There is greater safety in building connection than there is in remaining isolated.

Friendspiration: "The love in me calls out to the love
in others and can never be extinguished."

If the woman who wrote me the email was able to believe that flaws in others didn't automatically make her unsafe, or if she valued possible intimacy as greater than the fear of getting hurt, how might she have been willing to lean in to see if she could actually find more to trust in, not less?

Choosing My Courageous Truths

MY PERCEIVED FEARS	MY COURAGEOUS TRUTHS
I am afraid everyone might be passive-aggressive and selfish.	Well, either we all are, including me, which means we all need to figure out how to get along; or there are many people out there, like me, trying not to be this way, and I can find them.
They could hurt me.	No matter what they do or don't do, my value isn't diminished. I am safe. They might indeed disappoint me, but if they do then I will commit myself to forgiving them, as well as to healing anything in me that needs healing.

(All exercises in this book appear in *The Frientimacy Workbook*, which you can download at: www.Frientimacy.com.)

FOR REFLECTION: Add to the list in the Choosing My Courageous Truths sidebar what you believe is really at risk in you if you were to engage with people who might disappoint you. What are you most afraid of? What could you really lose? Then, next to each of those perceived losses or fears, write a statement of truth instead.

FOR PRACTICE: Can you think of a friendship that you walked away from perhaps prematurely? If so, recall what the situation was that brought you to leave and identify why you were most afraid. Can you imagine how you might replay it if you felt completely safe and without fear? Now, is there a relationship in your life you're tempted to withdraw from that you can lean in the way you did in your replay?

Redefining the Popular Sayings

In closing let's revisit the advice cited at the beginning of the chapter, but this time reinterpreted through a lens of compassion that, rather than blaming others, instead owns how the responsibility to grow and develop is on us.

"People inspire you, or they drain you. Pick wisely." I don't pick people; rather, I choose my response. I get to decide whether I am inspired or drained. I can be around someone who shines and then walk away drained by jealousy, or I can sit with someone who is chronically depressed and walk away inspired and grateful. My power doesn't mean I get to pick who is valuable—it means I get to pick whether I'm able to see the value in everyone.

"If their presence can't add value to your life, then their absence will make no difference." This is such a dangerous message. It's one thing to walk away; it's quite another to oppress and denigrate. Instead, I consider that if someone's presence doesn't add value to my life, that's because either I haven't taken the time to get to know her yet, or I haven't yet seen who I can become because of her. Look deeper.

"Surround yourself with only people who are going to lift you higher." In the closest circle of your life, I agree that this is a good ideal. We want to love each other well, and to create relationships that nurture, uplift, and empower. But ultimately it's not up to others to decide whether we lift higher or not; that's our call. Again, the onus to grow is on us, not others.

Worth Remembering

- Emotional health—a broad umbrella that can include such things as emotional intelligence, self-actualization, and spiritual growth—is a regularly fluctuating continuum, not a set yes-or-no determination.
- Let's freely acknowledge that we don't always present to our friends the most enlightened, healthy, and happy versions of ourselves—nor do they. The trick is to judge less, observe more, and continue working on ourselves.

- We inevitably have to interact with those who are hurting, jealous, and still growing. But when we choose to approach everyone with kindness, *we* grow in the process.

- We can further our own growth with five practices: owning our imperfections, assuming the best in others, trying to understand the needs of the other, changing our concept of "needy," and trusting that we are safe.

- Our goal is to create friendships that allow for imperfect actions—theirs and ours—without letting those actions threaten the friendship. It's with trust and ownership that we can deepen our frientimacy.

Next up: when jealousy and envy rear their ugly heads, threatening our frientimacy.

12

Obstacle to Intimacy #4: Jealousy and Envy

Or, The Fear *They're* Too Good

When we were kids, my sisters and I compared how many gifts under the Christmas tree awaited each of us. We complained when our cousin got one more horsey ride from our favorite uncle than we did. We pouted when our friend's mother let her have dessert after our mom told us we'd reached our sugar quota for the day. And we cried "Unfair!" when our friend earned more tickets than we did playing Skee-Ball at Chuck E. Cheese's. (As if lives succeeded or failed based on how many plastic spiders and erasers we walked away with!) I even remember feeling slighted at Baskin-Robbins when my sister counted more pink bubble gum balls in her scoop of ice cream than I did in mine. As children, we defined equality as having the same of everything—whether attention or possessions. Anything less was injustice.

As adults, we experience jealousy when our coworker is praised or promoted, when our romantic interest flirts with someone else, when our child bonds with another adult, or when everyone gushes over another volunteer's contribution when ours was just as important. We are envious when a family member loses weight more easily than we do, or when our Facebook friends seem to be living more exciting lives than we are. We are now old enough to know that "life isn't fair," so we can't run around calling foul every time someone gets something we don't have. But that doesn't stop us from sometimes fearing that our value is determined by how much praise, attention, rewards, possessions, and opportunities we receive—or don't.

GENTLE TRUTH: We can't enjoy intimacy if we begrudge others

Envy and jealousy are all about comparisons, and everything is a contest: how quickly we meet our romantic partners and how long we stay together, which cars we drive and what brands we wear, how brilliant our kids are, how satisfied we are with our careers, how much money we earn and how well off we'll be when we retire. And as is true in a contest, not everyone can win. Since competition implies scarcity, and no one wants to be left with the short end of the stick, it makes sense that we can feel anguish when someone has more than we do. But this is where it's crucial to define the difference between envy and jealousy.

Though many of us use these words interchangeably, they are in fact two distinct emotions. We feel *envy* when someone else has something we desire; we feel *jealousy* when we fear losing something, or someone, to someone else.

For example, when we see a photo on Facebook of our best friend out with other friends, feeling *jealousy* would mean we resent those other friends because we're afraid of losing her to people she likes better—whereas feeling *envy* would mean that we wished we'd been there as well, or that she had that much fun with us, or maybe that we want more friends in our lives. Distinguishing between the two is important because how we feel influences the way we respond. If we're jealous, then we might cling to our friend, get mad at her for betraying us, or try to compete with her new friends as if it were a case of "us versus them." If we're envious, then we'd probably feel a little lonely or insufficient or wish we knew how to attract additional friends.

When we learn to distinguish between jealousy and envy we can learn to recognize whether we need to 1) protect something that we fear losing, or 2) need to proactively seek something we desire. Not surprisingly, these two very different needs call for very different plans of actions.

I frequently observe two types of jealousy and two types of envy. Let's start with jealousy—the fear of losing someone or something we already have to someone else. There is "unreliable jealousy," caused by a loss we fear will happen, and "reliable jealousy," caused by a loss that is actually happening.

UNRELIABLE JEALOUSY: Fearing we will lose something—means we're responding from a place of fear and insecurity. Freaking out because our friend has other friends, we might convince ourselves that if she loves others she can't also love us, or that if she loves the others more she'll leave us. Unreliable jealousy can cause feelings of paranoia, delusion, and anxiousness, all of which can have less to do with the real circumstances than with some previous wound, extreme insecurity, broken trust, or a control obsession. Unreliable jealousy lies to us, telling us that relationships, possessions, or opportunities are being stolen from us. From this place we act with a defensiveness that is motivated by fear, propelled by the belief that someone is betraying us.

RELIABLE JEALOUSY: Perceiving we are in fact losing something is information, and amazing information at that! To sense that something we love is, indeed, being threatened means that our internal danger-detector is working effectively. The red flags of reliable jealousy invite us to examine our relationships with the intention of increasing trust, joy, and mutual benefit. And while possible loss and rejection are always painful to contemplate, it helps to distinguish what we are actually feeling. In the scenario of our friend's Facebook photo, reliable jealousy doesn't mean we want to deprive someone else of what she wants; it simply means we don't want to lose what we have. It's not that we don't want our friend to have other healthy and fabulous friendships—it's just that we're pained at the thought of losing the bond we have with her. Ultimately, reliable jealousy is motivated by love, fueled by a desire for both people to have more, not less. Clarifying this fact can single-handedly lead you toward a positive and productive solution.

Similarly, envy—the recognition that we want something that we lack—also has two different expressions. I call them "resenting envy" and "applauding envy." In discussing them, let's expand the Facebook scenario, this time having the posted photo be one taken when our friend took another trip to another idyllic locale—something we can't afford.

RESENTING ENVY: When we begrudge the other person for having what we want, not only are we pained that we don't have it, but we wish she didn't either. Sometimes we even feel angry with her for having what we want, faulting her for having it easier or devaluing her or the accomplishment with snarky comments or bitterness. So in our scenario, if we feel resenting envy we resent our friend for having the money, time, or courage to go on trips to far-off places. From this bitterness we're prone to criticize her for gallivanting around the world, denigrate the sacrifices she made in order to make the trip, or relish the stress awaiting her at work when she returns.

With APPLAUDING ENVY, while we may still feel a sting when we perceive another has what we want, we quickly acknowledge that we wouldn't want her to not have it. In owning our hunger, we also recognize that our friend having something we want doesn't prevent us from getting it, too. So when we see our friend's photos, instead of wishing that she hadn't been able to go on this trip, we acknowledge that we want to go on vacations, too—or at least that we want the feeling we think would come with such a vacation. By recognizing this feeling as information, we can ultimately feel inspired, not limited, by our friend's relationships, accomplishments, and opportunities.

Sitting with envy takes the courage to look at our lives and ask hard questions. What am I feeling? What information can I glean from this situation? What desire or longing in my soul does this tap for me, or symbolize to me? Am I envious of the actual circumstances or accomplishment, or just what they represent to me? Is there anything I want to do differently about my life now—do I need to make a courageous decision, or act from a different place? Or am I already moving toward this, and just need to show compassion to myself and trust the process?

Do you see the connection between the two types of jealousy and envy? One version focuses on *the other* (as someone who is to blame or who doesn't deserve what she has); the other version focuses on *the self* (acknowledging what I want to protect or hope to still experience).

It's super important to recognize that managing jealousy and envy is *our* issue, our opportunity to grow—especially since those emotions can be so problematic. According to the Frientimacy Survey, 54 percent of us admitted that being jealous negatively affected our friendships; that's a pretty significant number. So, while both jealousy and envy can be powerful and good forces in our lives, signaling what's important to us, we'll also want to ensure they remain productive and loving forces, not harmful and resentful ones.

COURAGEOUS ACTIONS: Five Practices for Cheering, Not Competing

Jealousy and envy are primarily internal feelings, often provoked by a craving for more contentment and confidence in our lives. When we pay attention to these feelings, they can help us keep perspective and give us the information to make wise decisions. But that doesn't mean we can't also benefit from discussing our feelings with those we trust: It so happens that relationships can be a perfect forum for practicing the very contentment and confidence we crave. In working *in* our relationships, we can learn how to both better celebrate others *and* move ourselves forward.

Here are five ways to encourage cheering instead of competing in our friendships:

When a friend announces she's pregnant, send a gift with a note of congratulations—even if you wish you were the one expecting a child. When she announces she's won a trip to Tahiti, tell her: "Have extra fun for me!" When your single pal gets hit on by five guys in one night—and you got zero—smile, and ask what perfume she wears. When your only friend says she's going out with coworkers again, recommend a restaurant they can try. When another mom boasts how relieved she is that her child got into an elite camp, marvel aloud what an amazing experience it will likely be.

Now, if that's not what you feel, you might think those responses are inauthentic—and that's okay. We all have a collection of voices in our heads, beliefs in our hearts, and aspects of our personalities that influence our every decision. I think of all these voices as the people on my team, sitting around my conference table, making their voices heard before every vote.

One is the voice of a toddler, who reliably stomps her feet, screaming how everything is unfair. Also present is the voice of your adolescent self, convinced she knows everything and ready to rebel against any perceived favoritism. And of course we have the ever-ready critic, railing about how inadequate and pathetic you are for not having what your friend has. So far, this is not exactly a meeting you want to be a part of. But fortunately you also have the voice of a wise woman, who speaks quietly and comfortingly. She assures you: "You are exactly as you are meant to be right now. You have so much to be grateful for, and you can trust your life to unfold with good gifts." Beside her is a voice of kindness, whose job it is to help us to love more, and to connect and bond with others. She says, "While our team works on the best plans for *our* future, we first need to respond to our friend with love and generosity."

And so, back to the baby announcement or the dance floor: As long as one person on the team in your head whispers the idea of kindness, you can express it to your friend with sincerity. Haven't we all at one point in time behaved the way the pouting toddler or the sarcastic teenager encouraged us to act, even when we felt divided? So we may as well encourage a few more of our wise voices to speak up more often—and determine which voices we let influence us. Your begrudging feelings are no more authentic than your feelings of kindness.

Friendspiration: "Expressing love is always an authentic gesture since love abides in me."

You head the board—you decide who you listen to. So cheer on your friend, give her a thumbs up, congratulate her accomplishments, pinch her baby's cheeks, and thank that good man of hers for treating her so well.

Plus, the more you cheer for your friend, the more likely it is that your friendship will not just survive, but thrive. As you encourage her, she will almost certainly cheer for your continued success as well. So cheer on! The love you spread will always come back to you.

FOR REFLECTION: Think of a situation that provokes your envy and try to identify all the different voices you can hear in your head. See the "Voices in My Head" worksheet on page 202 as you try to distinguish as many conflicting emotions as possible.

FOR PRACTICE: Who is one person you're struggling to cheer for right now? What is the nicest thing you could do to show her your genuine support and affirmation? Are you willing to do it?

The Voices in My Head

The Statements	The Identity	The Fear	The Need	The Value
What are you thinking?	What name do you give the voice expressing this thought? What does she look like?	What is this voice most afraid of?	What does this voice need in order to feel safe—so she can be most helpful?	If her needs were met, how could this part of me help create more intimacy?
"My friend thinks she's so much more amazing than she really is!"	She looks like one of those mean girls in high school who walk the halls putting everyone in their place. I'll call her the High School Bully.	This voice is afraid of feeling threatened, like she's losing her rank if someone else is impressive.	She needs to realize that she's not liked because she's in power but because of how others feel in her presence. She doesn't lose "popularity" or rank by belittling; she earns it by being likable.	She could be an influencer in the "high school halls" by being someone who affirms others instead of bullying them. She can help me realize that impressing people is far less helpful than relating to people is.

(All exercises in this book appear in *The Frientimacy Workbook*, which you can download at: www.Frientimacy.com.)

Practice #2: Befriend Those You Think "Have It All"

As you begin to realize that jealousy and envy are *your* feelings to own—not feelings to be blamed on someone else—you'll no longer need to avoid the people who previously made you feel threatened. You can prove this to yourself by seeking a friendship with the very type of woman who has often triggered your envy.

For starters, you might learn something important about what comes with what you *think* you crave. For example, let's say you're envious of a woman whose job title you want for yourself. You might end up learning that she works exceptionally long hours and has to spend weeks at a time away from her young children. Allowing yourself to get closer to those you'd previously avoided could reveal that no one lives without stress, fear, and sadness—and that their "plum" situations could include things you wouldn't relish in your life. As you get closer, you might see that, although she is walking *her* path, and much about that path may be beautiful and right for her, she also has her own insecurities and fears. Being reminded that there is no one who has "arrived"—that we're all still striving—can make us a little more compassionate and patient with ourselves.

Furthermore, even if her life looks more and more amazing the closer you get, there is much to be gained by being near women who have created lives that feed them. If you chose to learn from them rather than dismiss them, then some of what works for them may inspire you to really clarify your goals and desires, think positively, and take courageous actions toward your own intentions.

---

*Friendspiration: "Since success and happiness are
contagious, I hope my friends have tons of both."*

I know an infertile woman who for the longest time couldn't bear to be around women with young kids. Finally her envy brought her to a place where she realized she need not go through life avoiding babies just because she couldn't have one of her own. So she began befriending moms and offering to babysit and be present in the lives of their kids. By befriending the very women she had so long avoided, she turned her pain into a blessing.

When we are willing to practice holding our own worth in the presence of anyone we admire, we are able to expand our sense of worth.

FOR REFLECTION: Can you think of someone you know (or even just know on Facebook) who to your mind "has it all?" When you think of that person, what response do you typically feel? How might that response differ if you intentionally responded with Applauding Envy instead of Resenting Envy?

FOR PRACTICE: What is one action you can take today to encourage or cheer for that person who you feel has it all?

Practice #3: Express Empathy Regardless of the Circumstances

When we feel envious of someone whose circumstances seem better than our own, we are more susceptible to discounting her feelings within those circumstances. We might roll our eyes away from her fit physique when she complains about gaining weight, or lose patience when she complains about her boyfriend when we'd be thrilled to have a boyfriend as considerate as hers.

I remember listening to one of my friends stress about her family finances and all I could think was, "Give me a break! I could live ten years on what you have in savings right now!" It was nearly impossible for me to feel true concern for her or empathize with her fear, because all I could see was how much I wished I had what she had.

Friendspiration: "I want to be the kind of person who can empathize with anyone."

But empathy means tapping into the feelings of the other person, not imagining how we'd feel in the same situation. When we offer empathy to those we love it's important to stay with *her* feelings, remembering times *we've* felt the same way. My friend was stressed about not having enough money—a feeling I know intimately—so I could have used that moment as my practice ground for relating to her feelings rather than diminishing them. It doesn't matter if her bank-balance panic point has two more zeros than mine; the point is that we both know how it feels to worry about someday not having enough.

Insecurity is universal. So let's practice not only hearing our friends' complaints and fears, but also then validating them. Let our empathy derive from our shared feelings, regardless of the details.

FOR REFLECTION: What are some of the subjects—body image, finances, marriage, career achievements—that trigger your frustration when someone else "with more" complains about them? What feelings come up when you think of how what you don't have might negatively affect you? Remind yourself that others with different circumstances can experience this same fear or panic.

FOR PRACTICE: Do you have a friend who complains about a situation you'd prefer over your own? Can you think of a new supportive, empathetic response you could offer that acknowledges that you understand her feelings?

Practice #4: Tell Your Friends You've Envied Them

Deepening a friendship calls for learning to be friends in a variety of circumstances. It also calls for learning to talk about a variety of subjects, including our feelings. Envy needn't be off-limits in our conversations! Our brain will try to shame us into denying feelings of envy, as if such signaled weakness, labeling us as inadequate. But that's just our ego playing tricks on us. The truth is that envy is just a feeling, like sadness or fear; it's there to give us information, not to shame us.

With a close friend we can practice saying, "I am so absolutely proud of you for building up your business with such success, but I'd be lying if I didn't also admit that there's a tiny part of me that feels envious, too. Not the kind of envy that doesn't want your success, just the kind of envy that reminds me I want my work to matter, too!"

Or, perhaps we admit that our friend's happiness is interfering with our relationship in a negative way. For example, "You may have noticed that I pulled away a bit when you told me you're getting married. I want to apologize for that! When I reflected back on it, I realized I was undoubtedly acting from a place of both envy and jealousy. Jealousy because I started feeling like I was going to lose you, and our friendship matters so much to me. And envy because it reminds me that I so want to get married and I'm scared I'll never find someone who makes me feel the way Rob makes you feel. But I want you to know that I am aware of those feelings and I take responsibility for them. They aren't your fault at all! I truly am happy for you. I just wanted to explain my behavior so you didn't doubt how much I care about you."

Or perhaps we make a more casual admission: "Oh you look so good! I know you've been so committed to eating healthy and exercising. I am so envious of the results!"

Friendspiration: "I want friendships where we can talk about anything—including our feelings."

Being emotionally intelligent means we're capable of feeling and admitting to the entire range of our feelings. We need to practice talking about our feelings so as to remove any sense of shame from words that are simply part of the human experience. In so doing we can communicate to our friends that we welcome them to also be in touch with their feelings when they're around us.

FOR REFLECTION: Can you recall an incident when you felt jealous or envious about a friend? Now, imagine admitting your feelings to that friend: Would that be too scary to do? Let's say a friend felt the same about you: How would you feel if she admitted having those same feelings? Consider what you want in your friendships: Do you value honesty, vulnerability, and intimacy more than you fear making awkward announcements?

FOR PRACTICE: Imagine a scenario likely to occur in the future where you might feel jealousy. Plan in advance what sharing you might offer when it happens.

We live in a world where we dream of having a tribe—being part of a group of friends—and yet more often than not I see women hoard friends and act threatened when their friends hang out without her. We don't have to be in the middle of everything all the time. We can trust that different friends feed different needs at different times. We can trust that when we build enough love around us, there will be plenty to share with others.

And about your closest friend: Being a best friend is more about the quality of the relationship than the quantity of friends. "Best friend" doesn't mean "one-and-only friend"; it simply means the two of you have reached a level of trust and history and love. And both of you can do that with several people without diminishing your mutual love for each other. All of us are healthier and happier when we are supported and fed by several kinds of relationships, including those with our best friends. So when she establishes other friendships, we should see that as a sign that she's a healthy friend.

When you see photos of her on Facebook with other friends, leave encouraging comments, like "So glad you two had fun skiing!" When you meet her friends, whether you love them instantly or not, be magnanimous and kind, showing your appreciation that they're in her life. When your friend suggests inviting someone else to an activity you two are scheduled to share, take it as a compliment that she wants her friends to meet you. When a birthday or wedding approaches, be the one who reaches out to co-plan a party. Anyone who loves our friend and helps her heart feel supported is a friend of ours. We're not in competition with her; we are on the same side, on a team of women who love the same person. Practice seeing your friend's friends as your teammates!

Friendspiration: "There is enough love to share."

And if your friend doesn't have other friends, then introduce her to some of yours. Trust that there is enough love to share, and that if she bonds with one of them it doesn't mean either of them loves you any less. Be known as someone who supports friendship happening all around you.

FOR REFLECTION: Can you recall an incident when you felt less than happy to learn about a friend having "friend fun" without you? Do you remember how you felt? Is there anything you could have done to feel more at peace in that situation?

FOR PRACTICE: How many of the girlfriends of your closest friends can you name? What could you do to get to know some of them better, or to better support their friendships with your shared friend?

Celebrating Growth

It's so easy to feel jealousy or envy and react out of fear. Our default reaction to a threat, real or perceived, is either to retreat or to attack. But we can choose to react differently. We can celebrate our friends and acquaintances just for being who they are—without blaming them for how we feel about ourselves when their stars are shining. None of the choices they make, the awards they win, or the happiness they feel diminishes who we are in any way.

The more often we practice cheering through envy, the easier it will be to do so when we bump into the women we don't yet know but could someday love: women we perceive as competitors; women who we think have it all; women who are beautiful, famous, creative, successful, or wealthy; women who courageously run for office or advocate for important causes; women we're tempted to criticize because they do something differently; women who seem to enjoy the spotlight more than we think they should; women who have ambitions or goals that we don't fully understand; women who are doing what we wish we were doing.

The world needs far more women of strength and purpose. Let's applaud them for their courage, knowing we only gain from the progress.

Worth Remembering

- We feel *envy* when someone else has something we desire; we feel *jealousy* when we fear losing something, or someone, to someone else.

- Distinguishing which emotion we feel influences the way we respond. We could either 1) work to protect something that we fear losing, or 2) decide to proactively seek something we desire.

- Both jealousy and envy can be powerful and good forces in our lives, signaling what's important to us. We just need to ensure they remain productive and loving, not harmful and resentful.

- We can further our own growth in this area with five practices: by cheering even when we're not feeling cheerful; by befriending those we think "have it all"; by expressing empathy regardless of the circumstances; by telling our friends we've envied them; and by supporting our friends to have other friends.

- When we are willing to practice holding our own worth in the presence of anyone we admire, we are able to expand our sense of worth.

- Let's practice hearing our friends' complaints and fears and then validating them. We want our empathy to derive from our shared feelings.

- We can trust that different friends feed different needs at different times. We will build enough love around us that there is plenty to share with others.

Next up: when *we're* the object of jealousy—and how that impacts our frientimacy.

13

Obstacle to Intimacy #5: Holding Ourselves Back

Or, The Fear They Think *We're* Too Good: Being the Object of Jealousy

few years ago a childhood memory surfaced. We were in the kitchen in our little yellow house in Denver, and my mom was oohing and ahhing over a drawing my younger sister had completed. She suggested my sister would enjoy signing up for an art class. I jumped into the conversation, excitedly telling Mom I thought I'd enjoy that class, too.

My mom said, "Let this be just your sister's thing, Shasta. You have plenty of other interests." What I heard was: "She can't become her best self if you're there, too. You take over, do everything bigger and louder, think you can do everything better. In order for her to emerge, we need you to back off."

I carried far into adulthood the belief that if I shine too much I prevent my sister from shining. I grew up with an unconscious belief that I was responsible for how my sister felt. Even now a misunderstood version of the "golden rule" whispers in my head that I should never do anything that makes someone else feel bad. And I'd never want to make anyone feel bad! But what if just being the best version of *myself* makes someone else feel bad about herself—then what?

So, while I was lucky to believe that I *could* be anything I wanted, somewhere along the way I came to think I shouldn't *look* like I wanted it. I felt I was expected to undersell my contribution, display false modesty, and pretend I didn't care for the accolades of my accomplishments—all while giving full credit to others.

I'm a people-pleaser, so it was tempting to choose popularity over power. I'd rather be liked than be envied or judged, so I strove to not be seen as ambitious. But at the same time, I also wanted to actualize my best self. So I became a pendulum, swinging back and forth between shining and dimming, succeeding and apologizing, ever-conscious of how I appeared to others and how that made them feel.

GENTLE TRUTH: We can't enjoy intimacy if we stay small instead of shining big

In an article titled "Facing Up to the Female Power Conundrum," *Fortune* editor Patricia Sellers wrote: "Women can be powerful. Women can be likable. Being both is hard to do."

There's a positive correlation for men between power and likability, meaning the two qualities frequently go hand in hand. Women, however, often have to choose between the two: When in positions of leadership, power, or influence, women frequently encounter jealousy, competition, skepticism, and criticism. Unfortunately, both genders are far more comfortable with seeing men be the ones who act aggressively, powerfully, and decisively.

I have felt the most friction with my female connections during times of greatest visibility in my career. For example, there was a marked difference in how other women reacted to me during different phases of my life: such as when I presided as student association president in college, cohosted a small TV show in my early twenties, or spoke around the country—compared to times when I was depressed after my divorce, uncertain about my career direction, or honest about my paltry finances.

In times of the former, I felt criticized; in the latter, I felt comforted. I quickly learned that I preferred women's encouragement to their judgment.

Even in writing this chapter I feel slightly worried about what everyone will think. Will you think I'm vain? Do I sound pretentious? Am I less relatable and likable now? Most women aren't used to talking with other women about our ambitions, our dreams, our potential, and our success.

But I'm going to guess that many of you know the feeling: You downplay how awesome you think your kids are so it doesn't look like you're bragging, decide not to tell your friends how much you really adore your husband since they don't seem to feel the same about theirs, hesitate to wear an outfit that's "too much" because you don't want to appear to be trying to get attention, or sound more worried about your finances than you really are to try to relate better with everyone else's primary concern.

It was mentioned earlier that the majority of us report feeling jealous of our friends, and that such negatively impacts our friendships. In addition, in the Frientimacy Survey one out of every five women felt being the *object* of jealousy had a negative impact. Some of the comments included:

- "I don't want to say that I can only hang out with other women who have wealth, but I'm getting tired of apologizing for it or feeling guilty that I've earned it."

- "Just because I was born beautiful doesn't mean I don't want friends. But for some reason most women are cold to me before they even meet me."

- "They say it's lonely at the top—and I can attest that's true."

- "My friend who always struggles with her weight almost seems to despise me for being naturally skinny."

Reading those pleas for connection sinks my heart.

Being the object of jealousy is not an enviable position, as it is often isolating—leaving us feeling we have only two options: to dim our lights in order to connect with others, or to shine while acting as if impervious to others' opinions, as if we didn't give a damn. I call it "dimming or damning," and both are problematic, diminishing not just our identities but also our contributions to the world. "Dimming" robs us all of that contribution, and "damning" can poison that contribution, leaving a "gift" that's had all the love sucked out of it.

"Dimmers," usually subconsciously, choose approval over achievement: downplaying promotions, brushing off compliments, shrugging as if their contributions were nothing. They don't want to make anyone feel bad. They want to be liked. They want to fit in. It may stop them from writing books, painting art, traveling the world, taking risks, or being an amazing and visionary leader.

If a career in the arts isn't viewed as appropriate to their tribe, they'll pursue a "real job" instead. If being beautiful is threatening to their friends, they'll work to hide it. If being competitive, influential, or commanding is seen as "trying too hard," then they'll pretend they don't possess those strengths. If having the luxury of not being tethered to the grindstone puts a target on their backs, they'll feel guilty for having the privilege.

Of course, some cases of jealousy—like for being skinny, wealthy, or popular—might not seem to be shying away from a contribution exactly, but they are all the same. Anytime we feel guilty for our privileges or shamed for who we are, we become a little less self-confident or self-honoring. Most of us probably couldn't even pinpoint what we don't do out of concern for what others would think—we've simply become accustomed to not putting our necks on the line.

"Damning" is no less destructive. In choosing achievement over relationships, we're likely to drive over people, hold others to impossible standards, and come across as cold or uncaring—even when such couldn't be further from the truth. "Damners" can in fact care so much they have to stop listening to their hearts, believing they're better off hiding their vulnerabilities under lock and key. The path of lonely success is tragic—especially given how it's not achievements but having meaningful relationships that leads us to health and happiness. Though "damners" can believe they're shining their lights, anything done without love in its soul will not in truth gift this world.

There has to be a way for us to shift the "likability and power" conundrum. No one wins by being either the subject or the object of envy. We need a world of women who feel they can both leave their mark *and* do so from a place of support and love.

We need a world of women who feel they can leave their
mark—and feel supported and loved in the process.

COURAGEOUS ACTIONS: Five Practices for Shining While Encouraging Others

It's not our job to shine less just to prevent others from feeling jealous; the world needs every positive contribution. But at the same time it *is* our responsibility to not let our shining distance us from the love we seek. Giving ourselves permission to shine will take a great deal of practice, and even more courage. Doing it while inviting others to shine with us calls for a level of maturity and self-worth that far too few of us have mastered. But we can do this. To follow are five practices for encouraging us all to shine. First, we start with ourselves.

Practice #1: Foster Self-Reflection

The opening montage in the movie *He's Just Not That into You* perfectly showcases how much effort we go through trying to avoid saying hurtful truths to our friends. Instead of saying, "Maybe he's not calling you back because he doesn't see a future relationship with you," we're more likely to wonder out loud if he's traveling, or perhaps he lost your number, or he's working up his courage, or some such gentle letdown. One character says it this way: "We are all programmed to believe that if a guy acts like a total jerk that means he likes you."

We do a similar thing when discussing female friendships as well, just with a different go-to line. For example, a woman I know, "Jennifer," once described to a group of us how a friend made passive-aggressive statements about how she spends her money. In a voice clearly relaying the pinched tone of hurt, Jennifer told us: "Instead of getting excited about my new car, she almost seemed upset at me when she annoyingly mumbled something about how leases aren't smart financial moves." Everyone dutifully jumped in: "She just wishes she had as much money as you do. She's just jealous."

Such words can feel good—especially to our egos (which aren't all that interested in self-growth and would frankly prefer to be continually told we're awesome). But being given a not-guilty plea doesn't *make* someone innocent.

Maybe Jennifer's friend is jealous, but maybe she isn't. Maybe the friend values different things, and can't understand why someone would lease a car instead of buying a used one. Hers might be an unfair judgment, but it's not necessarily jealousy. Or, maybe Jennifer spends her own money pretty thoughtlessly and would benefit from looking at why she gets defensive about her spending habits. Or, maybe Jennifer bought the car hoping it would make her cooler—and felt crushed when someone wasn't wowed. Or, maybe these two friends have some unmet needs and unspoken frustrations between them, rifts that would come out over any subject, not just this one.

I don't know. And, unfortunately, neither will Jennifer, as long as she simply concludes that jealousy took down another victim. We do no one any favors when we assume jealousy is always the culprit. More important, when we seek to assuage our hurt feelings we often sidestep valuable opportunities to examine our lives, to ask questions of our friends, and to grow deeper.

How? Well, what if, instead of shutting down or turning away, Jennifer had leaned in just a bit and asked, "What do you mean by that?" Or what if she said, "The last few times I've bought something I've felt like it's hard for you to be excited for me. Is that what you're feeling?" Or, perhaps the hardest of all, what if she had sat with the discomfort long enough to inquire of herself: "What about her statement bothers me? Why is it sticking with me? What is getting mirrored back to me?"

There's another reason to not sidestep. Every time we hear and believe that women are jealous of us, we set ourselves up to fear that no one can be friends with us. In other words, we further cement our brain synapses to suspect exactly what we *don't* want: that we'll be lonely because we shine, or that we need to dim ourselves in order to be liked. Neither option is okay with me.

Friendspiration: "I value personal growth
greater than I value coddling my ego."

So, what was the deal in *He's Just Not That into You*? One of the guys tells the woman that if a guy doesn't call her back it means he doesn't want to. End of story. He promises her that all the excuses her friends are coming up with are bogus—because an interested guy wouldn't let anything get in his way. In other words, the woman's friends helped to mask a truth she didn't want to face.

What if we did the same: stopped allowing ourselves to use the "she's just jealous" excuse, and instead tried to examine our own truths? Let's be women who refuse to assume what others are feeling or thinking—whether they're in the room with us or not.

FOR REFLECTION: Can you think of a time when you brushed something off with a comment like "she's just jealous"? Imagine that is only one explanation out of ten possible options. What are the other nine possible explanations? Write them down.

FOR PRACTICE: Can you think of someone in your life right now you've often assumed is jealous of you? If you pinpoint one or two specific incidents where you've felt that, can you imagine offering her a conversation starter similar to the Jennifer one cited above? (Were she to have said to her friend: "The last few times I've bought something I've felt like it's hard for you to be excited for me. Is that what you're feeling?") In what ways could you ask your friend what she's really feeling? Can you be open to initiating a conversation about what triggers her words or behaviors?

Practice #2: Focus Less on Good Impressions and More on Good Relations

There was a time when I couldn't invite friends over for dinner without wanting to impress them. I would have undoubtedly told you, with sincerity, how much I enjoyed my creative menu planning, the yummy recipe making, and the beautiful table setting. But in all honesty, within that intention was also a desire to wow as the perfect hostess.

Then a friend joked that she could never have me over because she felt she couldn't compete; I had set the bar too high. And in a flash I realized that deep down, under the desire to impress, my desire to feel connected was stronger. Those two outcomes that had seemed inextricable—being impressive and being connected—suddenly felt oppositional, even incompatible.

I had mistakenly believed that impressing others was what I was supposed to do—basically, that the way to get friends was to get people to like me, and for them to like me I had to impress them. But in so doing I had overlooked the fact that my hard-won efforts had created an intimacy gap—which was the exact opposite of what I wanted.

Now, it's easy to say that my friend "should" have had the confidence to not compare, or that it's not my problem if others feel small in my presence. Both statements hold fragments of truth. But luckily my friend's admission alerted me to the deeper truth: Being connected is more fulfilling than being admired.

This was years ago. Today, I still invite friends to dinner. I still plan perhaps-impressive menus, and I still cook yummy food because this *is* one of the ways I like to express my love. But now, instead of spending much of my time in my kitchen, I spend way more time at my table: inquiring about my friends' lives, listening to their stories, and affirming what I see in them.

I also serve spruced-up store-bought stuff, not just homemade; I intentionally don't clean my house the day of; and every visitor has at least once been served on paper plates. Plus, far more important than not taking myself as a hostess too seriously is my desire that all who walk into my home will leave feeling better about who they are.

Which, perhaps surprisingly, I find more fulfilling than I found all my earlier perfect quintessential parties. Perhaps this is because people who feel loved are more capable of returning it, and feeling their love lends a beautiful shine to the sink piled with dishes—or the compost bag holding all those paper plates.

In our attempts to be Super Woman, we seem to think that other women will like us more the more amazing we are, but in doing that we can forget that "amazing" can be intimidating—and intimidating is more distancing than bonding. There is nothing wrong with being the best yogi in the class, the trendiest girl in school, the friendliest mom on the block, or the most successful salesperson in the department—unless we're doing it *because* we want to feel loved. Being great at what we do is one thing, confusing that with our value is another. How tragic if our underlying need—to bond with others—is left unmet because our overcompensating need to impress kept them at arm's length.

Friendspiration: "I let go of the need to impress and choose to look for ways to relate and connect."

I wish I could say I never have the urge to impress people anymore, but that would not be true. What is true is that many of the things we think we need to do or be in order to win the admiration of others usually masks a yearning to be liked and accepted. If we could hear it as such, we'd be far more successful in getting the love we want.

This isn't to say play smaller, cater to the insecurities of others, or feel responsible for how others feel. Indeed, the answer isn't to stop being impressive—unless it's masking the fact that it's connection we actually crave. Rather, the answer is to keep the focus on connecting and relating to others rather than focusing on the heroics we think will earn us that chance to connect. Why go the long way around trying to impress when we can just get straight to the point of loving each other?

FOR REFLECTION: Ask yourself: "Where am I most tempted to impress or try too hard? What motivates that? Is there an underlying insecurity? What would it look like if I were to focus on directly inviting love rather than trying to earn it by being amazing?"

FOR PRACTICE: For me, occasionally using paper plates for dinner with friends was a small way to practice letting go of the need to impress. What can you do to practice connecting more than wowing?

Practice #3: Find Peace with Not Eclipsing Others

This one follows conceptually from my lessons in connecting vs. impressing. In the previous practice we worked to identify more of *what* we do; here the challenge is to better understand *why* we can need to be the brightest light in the room—and to find peace with no longer needing to eclipse others.

Should you go this route your ego will understandably panic because it thinks that what makes you special is being the best or the only, and so to benefit the "competition," as it were, would be social suicide. But your inner wisdom will know that you can have it all—success, friends, and successful friends—as long as you come to realize how your value, in all its uniqueness, can readily withstand the presence of additional bright lights. To reach that realization you have to deeply understand what it is that makes you special—indeed, what it is that makes you loveable.

Those who find this challenging often believe, perhaps because of the specific kudos they receive, that their specialness derives from excelling in just one or two areas, and so to seem less bright in comparison can feel like being diminished. If this describes you, know that those areas of kudos are not what makes you *you*. Go back to Chapter 9, "Doubting Our Self-Worth," and commit to really getting to know yourself. Sometimes it's those of us who have been the object of jealousy that most suffer with fragile self-esteem, as we believe our worth is hinged upon something that could change.

But our worth is not conditional. We each have an individual essence—something far deeper than our personality, our looks, or our successes—that people experience when they are with us. It's *who* we are. The trick is remembering that how others experience us isn't how we experience ourselves—because we don't know what it's like to stand in our own presence. How I show up and contribute will look vastly different than how you do, even if we have the exact same job or privilege. We owe it to ourselves, and those we're in relationship with, to see just how different we each are—even when another "competing" bright light is nearby.

Once we're able to see that our gift isn't something outside, but something inside us, our eyes will be better able to see that everyone has an unmatched quality of his or her own. We each have different legacies and resources; we each make a valuable contribution.

And, once we understand it's our essence that makes us appealing, we can loosen our grip on that which we thought we needed in order to win others. Because to believe that it's our success that makes us lovable ensures that we chase our ambitions for all the wrong reasons. If what we want are people who love us no matter what, then it's our job to trust them to love *us*, not our achievements. How? By releasing our hold on the one thing we think we must be or do in order to win and retain affection.

Friendspiration: "I am the only 'me' out there, so no one is my competitor."

If you don't believe you're up to the task, then you'll never really be willing to fan the flames of others. You can give lip service to being a cheerleader or occasionally affirm those around you, but they will feel your limitations, and you likely won't secure the love you crave.

This path may be difficult for some of us to pursue, but we truly can be our best only when we can relax and *still* feel loved.

FOR REFLECTION: What words describe your essence? Imagine you are an animal or element in nature, and write a few paragraphs embodying your experience: What do you enjoy doing? What do you feel? What energy do you hold? After free-flow writing, go back and circle words and phrases that jump out at you. For example, let's say several people choose "water" as their essence; that water can be embodied differently by different people, whether they feel like gentle raindrops, flowing rivers, or mighty ocean waves. Some of us are purifying and healing, while others might be agents of change or inspiring.

FOR PRACTICE: What is one area of your life where you receive lots of kudos and enjoy being successful? When can you practice affirming others in this area without diminishing yourself? What would that look like?

Practice #4: Encourage Others to Shine

If we have friends we believe are jealous of us, we have a special opportunity to continue shining while also encouraging them to shine as well. And though it's their job to shine, not ours, we can help fan their flames. How? We can cheer for them, affirm them, and sing their praises when they feel doubt.

I'm a part of a group of nine amazing, kickass women who've met every month for the past three years to support and encourage each other in continuing our contributions to the world. We've undoubtedly all been jealous of each other at one time or another! And yet, what I admire about this group is that, while we persist in sharing our insecurities and practice asking each other for help, we also demand that every person owns her greatness. We don't want anyone backing down or dimming.

An important aspect of our group is that we don't simply cheer for each other as things come up—we also invoke each other to shine in our presence. We are proactive, not just reactive; we play offense, not just defense. So that means we ask questions like "What's energizing in your life right now?" Or, "What are some of the highlights of your summer?" Or, "Tell me something that you've done recently that made you feel proud."

In this way we gift our friendships by offering permission to shine in our presence, to choose happiness, and to love whom we were created to be. We create a safe place for us all to practice *not* minimizing our successes, *not* downplaying our ambitions, and *not* apologizing for our awards. And when one of us deprecates her contribution, we stop her and invite her to instead own her awesomeness, saying something like "That's not true! Tell us again what your boss said about your work last week." When one of us brushes off a compliment, we will tease her and say: "Try again, and this time just say thank you." If one of us shrinks in any way, we step up and say: "Not on my watch. When I'm on your team, you're expected to stand in your worth."

Friendspiration: "May I graciously receive affirmation and generously pass it on."

We practice being one safe place in this world where we are cherished for being our best. We ask about what brings us joy, how we're using our talents, and what parts of our lives feel successful. And in giving permission to each other to shine, we in turn give it to ourselves.

It's a beautiful thing to learn how to receive accolades or privileges rather than downplaying or dismissing them—but it's an even greater thing to learn how to pay it forward. Arrogance isn't believing we're amazing; arrogance is forgetting that everyone else is, too. We want to appreciate how others see us shine and then give that gift to others as well.

FOR REFLECTION: Do you fan the flames of your friends? On a scale of 1–10, with "10" being the best, how would you rate yourself as such? If you wanted to raise that number, what might you do?

FOR PRACTICE: Can you name a friend who often dismisses her success, downplays her awesomeness, or focuses too much on what isn't working? Write down some ways you can encourage her to not just shine but also to own her strengths—and practice discussing them with you. Note that this isn't about complimenting her; it's about invoking her to "compliment" herself!

Practice #5: Invite Others to Your Team

Many of us are almost hardwired to feel some sense of guilt or indebtedness about receiving from others, whether we're offered tangible gifts or intangible assistance. I think that underlying this response is a fear that we're weak if we need help—and we certainly don't want to appear weak. We are far more comfortable with being needed than we are with having needs.

Being raised by a single mom, I got an extra dose of the "You never really can count on anyone" message. My rite of passage for turning twelve was doing my own laundry, opening a small checking account (for buying my own clothes and entertainment with my allowance), and helping put dinner on the table. My mother believed that her job above all others was to teach me how to be independent, to take care of myself.

Unfortunately, whether one subscribes to thinking *"The only person you can depend on is yourself"* or *"Loneliness is the price of success,"* either way, we're barricading ourselves from intimacy. If you see yourself in this picture, know that if we are to increase intimacy we are charged with banding together, and that means not going it alone. Which means that we not only practice including others in our perceived prosperity but that we also practice being the ones who express how others can help us. We invite others to be part of our team.

If we think someone might be jealous of us, then we have the awesome opportunity of inviting her into our world, whether we do so subtly or blatantly. Welcome her to be a part of the team, to play a role, to share credit, or to enjoy our winnings with us.

For example, a few possibilities:

- If a friend is jealous that you have kids, see if she wants to be more involved with them. Bestow her as an aunt; affirm her involvement.
- If a friend is jealous that you *don't* have kids, have her pick a date when you can whisk her away for a responsibility-free weekend.
- If a friend is jealous that you started your own business, offer to help her start hers, or ask her for advice, letting her help add value to yours.
- If a friend is jealous that you have money coming out of your ears, be the friend who says, "I'm treating you today. You give to me in so many other ways; this is one way I can give to you. Please let me."

Some may have a harder time asking for the support we need, but doing so is essential to building frientimacy. As one woman articulated: "I have found that the 'need' to meet others' expectations of me being 'strong' hinders my ability to be vulnerable." But, in fact, we can demonstrate inner strength by admitting that we also have needs.

And one of those needs is perhaps needing friends who can celebrate us! When addressing issues of jealousy, we can ask for our friends' support in celebrating our happiness. There is something about saying to a friend, "I need you to help me celebrate this success," or, "It would mean so much to me to have your support in this choice" that speaks to her highest self. In other words, our willingness to expose our vulnerabilities in requesting greater depth from our friends amounts to a win-win for all of us.

Friendspiration: "I don't want to do life alone—I want to share my success and needs with others."

So, how might this look? Here are a few examples from my life:

- A friend in one of my groups texted all of us: "I find out this afternoon if my project gets nominated for an Emmy. I'm nervous! Please pray for me!!!!"

- Another friend confided to a small group of us in my living room: "I feel a wee bit uncomfortable to tell you all this since I know taxes hit you all hard, but I hope you're still willing to celebrate with me that I got the promotion!"

- A friend told me over tea: "Sometimes I feel like I'm not supposed to be this proud of how much my art is selling. I'm still wrapping my head around the fact that my inspiration is impacting people. Would you be willing to keep your eye on me to make sure that I don't sabotage myself or take it for granted?"

- And when working on my own projects (like this book) I ask my friends to celebrate with me all the steps along the way because it's important to savor each success.

And what do you think were the responses to all these requests? "Of course!"

People *want* to support each other. Gift your friends with intimacy by sharing with them how they can best support you.

FOR REFLECTION: Which is more difficult for you: to share what you want and need with others, or to practice including others in your perceived success? Why do you think that is? What would it take for you to be willing to practice doing more of both?

FOR PRACTICE: Think of a friend you'll see soon; decide one thing you want to share with her about something you're proud of or excited about. How can you share it in such a way that asks her for the response you want?

Shining Our Lights

We sat in a small living room in Noe Valley, five women—new friends, really—considering starting a weekly girls group. As our conversation turned to sharing what we most sought in the year ahead, I almost changed what I planned to say. It felt like too big of an ask, too presumptuous, too awkward. But then I just blurted it out—I needed their commitment that they'd be there for me, not just through any impending crisis, but also through any forthcoming success.

The words tumbling from my mouth felt strange to me.

Though there's a lot of friendship language around "being there" through our ups and downs—we seem to know better what's expected of us during the downs. We know that after breakups we're supposed to bring ice cream and watch chick flicks, that births call for casseroles and diaper changes in the midst of sleep deprivation, and that mean bosses deserve some well-chosen potent epithets. We know how to show up with empathy when we see their pain; when they're down, we know to pull them up. But when they're up, we aren't always as sure about what our roles should be; we have to resist any desire to bring them down. It's in moments like these that woman earn reputations as being catty, judgmental, and jealous.

So the five of us vowed we would work to support each other in being our best. We promised we'd be a safe place to share success, joys, and growth. And we vowed to practice on each other.

This made me feel more powerful than I'd ever felt before. And while my life didn't yet hold the triumph of the success I sought, I believed these women would have my back rain or shine—and they have, and still do.

Since then, we have all chosen (even when it's perhaps not our first impulse) to cheer for each other regardless of the circumstances. That means even the woman still reeling from a horrible breakup learns to cheer when her friend gets engaged. It means one of us might launch a successful business while another faces imminent financial loss. It means one friend will have the baby that another wants but may not ever have. And all this means we continue to hold to the belief that we are better people when we step out of *our* insecurity and into our *friend's* happiness.

We women may not be able to single-handedly solve the myriad issues we encounter in our culture: the media bias, the gender inequality, the impulsive temptation to view each other as competitors. But in our own way—perhaps small, perhaps not—we can offer each other friendship, friendship that can be sustained through whatever ambitions we choose to pursue. We can show up in ways that prove we don't have to choose between likability and accomplishment. And in the moments when another woman's joys turn our skin green, we can remember that she is someone's friend, if not also our own. She deserves our respect as much as we ourselves deserve it.

I choose to own both my power and keep my friends. I may not win any popularity contests, but I will at least walk in this world giving that which I want to someday receive. So I will choose to give other women, all of them, that same gift, believing that the thoughts I hold about them will shape the thoughts I have about myself. I want for them what I want for me.

Marianne Williamson says it best in *A Return to Love: Reflections on the Principles of "A Course in Miracles"*:

> Your playing small does not serve the world. There is nothing enlightened about shrinking so that other people won't feel insecure around you. We are all meant to shine, as children do. . . . As we let our own light shine, we unconsciously give other people permission to do the same. As we are liberated from our own fear, our presence automatically liberates others.

Worth Remembering

- Much of what we think we need to do or be in order to win the admiration of others usually masks a yearning to be liked and accepted. If we could hear it as such, we'd be far more successful in getting the love we want.

- Though it's our friends' job to shine, not ours, we can help fan their flames by cheering for them, affirming them, and singing their praises when they feel doubt.

- When we seek to assuage our hurt feelings, we often sidestep valuable opportunities to examine our lives, to ask questions of our friends, and to grow deeper.

- We can practice being vulnerable when we share what we want and need, and practice including others in our perceived prosperity.

- We are better people when we step out of *our* insecurity and into our *friend's* happiness.

Last Step: measuring our growth.

Conclusion

Three Ways to Measure Our Growth

Like little girls marking their height on the wall, or like women hoping the scale registers the change in weight they desire—we all know the feeling of wanting to see progress. Or, consider efforts to strengthen our physique: It's so gratifying to finally be able to touch your toes, to eventually lift heavier weights, or to run farther or faster than we could before.

In this book we've talked about relationships being the health clubs for our souls—where we work out and grow our emotional and relational health. The trouble is, in our personal growth gyms success can be harder to measure. So I wanted to end our journey together by sharing three ways I regularly measure my growth.

Tracking Relationship Growth: The Frientimacy Triangle

Far too often we track our relationship health by how many friends we have, how much we like them, how long we've known each other, or how much we have in common. While all those factors can feel important, the truth is that none of them actually measures whether those friendships are healthy, sustainable, and deep.

As we saw with the Frientimacy Triangle, a much better way to track the health of our friendships is to measure our positivity, consistency, and vulnerability with others. Our goal is frientimacy with a few people, which means moving toward the top of the Frientimacy Triangle with chosen friends. Everyone else we know and love will exist at various levels of the Triangle.

So one of the ways I measure the health of my friendships is to maintain for each friend a three-part ranking, considering on a scale from 1–10 how much *I* think we practice positivity, consistency, and vulnerability in our friendship. Note, though, that this isn't about evaluating my *friends*, but about evaluating the *relationships* with those friends. This says nothing about who they are or how amazing they are; it simply acknowledges what patterns exist between us at this time. And neither is the goal to have everyone score a 9 or 10! Most of us don't need more than a few friends with whom we can be painstakingly honest and with whom we feel so committed we're willing to go through any conflict or disappointment. The truth is that a lot of our joy can come from friends who rank somewhere in the 3–8 range. Someone who is a "4" can be a lovely lunch date once a month, someone fun to go out dancing with, or someone at the office who makes the day more bearable. The goal is just to see the range of my current friendships so I can make decisions about where I might like to pursue more growth.

Sample Frientimacy Chart					
Friendship	**Positivity Ranking**		**Consistency Ranking**		**Vulnerability Ranking**	
	3		5		1	
	Preferred Positivity Ranking?	Steps I can take to get there?	Preferred Consistency Ranking?	Steps I can take to get there?	Preferred Vulnerability Ranking?	Steps I can take to get there?
JANE	5	Try to schedule something new and fun to do together	5	I feel good about how often we get together.	5	Clearly we have a lot of room to grow in this area! I need to be more intentional about asking her questions, and willing to reveal more.

	1		4		4	
	Preferred Positivity Ranking?	Steps I can take to get there?	Preferred Consistency Ranking??	Steps I can take to get there?	Preferred Vulnerability Ranking?	Steps I can take to get there?
	6		5		7	
	Preferred Positivity Ranking?	Steps I can take to get there?	Preferred Consistency Ranking?	Steps I can take to get there?	Preferred Vulnerability Ranking?	Steps I can take to get there?
(All exercises in this book appear in *The Frientimacy Workbook*, which you can download at: www.Frientimacy.com.)						

In *The Frientimacy Workbook* you'll find a blank chart like the one in the sidebar that you can use to evaluate the friendships in your life. Once you've rated just the three frientimacy requirements for each (hold off on noting your preferred rankings and further steps), ask yourself:

- What feels good or gratifying as I look at my chart? What can I celebrate?

Next, revisit the chart, this time filling in the preferred rankings for each frientimacy requirement. In doing this, ask yourself:

- Which friendships scored differently from what I wish they were? What would be their ideal scores? What would it take to change those numbers?

- Which friendships might surprise me if I were to focus on them a bit more? Which of the three actions would I most need to give to that relationship to make the biggest difference?

- Which friendships might I need to come to peace with? In other words, what hasn't changed much despite all my efforts? Could I appreciate those friendships for what they are? What would that look like?

- What feels discouraging or concerning to me? Where do I want to see improvement? What would improvement look like to me?

- What advice would I offer myself based upon these answers?

Next, see what actions you might want to pursue in order to further your hopes for each friendship. Feel free to add these to the "Steps I can take to get there?" column. (Note: in the next section I discuss expanding vulnerability, so feel free to leave the Vulnerability next-step cells blank for now.) Be sure to also set a date when you'll reevaluate your progress. The eventual goal is to have our assessments reflect our desires: moving certain relationships as high as they can go, knowing how to address or rethink any relationship that feels stuck, and being grateful for all the other relationships and their contributions to your life.

TRACKING COURAGE GROWTH: The Vulnerability Compass

"Are you vulnerable?" As we saw in Five Practices for Expanding Vulnerability from Chapter 7, the answer to that question isn't a simple "yes" or "no." Being willing to live in our own skin, feel our worth no matter how others respond, pursue the connections that matter to us, and continue to reveal ourselves in deeper ways all take tremendous courage. While of course some of these actions will come easier to some of us than to others, know that they all get easier with practice.

As for myself, because vulnerability speaks to both my ability to accept myself and to show myself to others, it's one of the most important areas for me to be painstakingly honest about. I want to be able to say that my willingness to risk in the name of connection is continually expanding. With each new year I want to believe I will become more and more willing to value intimacy more than I value self-protection. I draw the vulnerability compass and rank myself 1–10 in each of the five areas of vulnerability. I personally want to expand my territory to be as big as possible, reflecting my willingness to go to great lengths to deepen relationships. To do that I reflect at length on my progress within the five vulnerability acts, writing out answers to questions like the following.

- *Knowing myself*: "How easy is it for me to own what I'm feeling? How often do I practice telling others my real feelings? How often do I ask for what I need?"

- *New activities*: "Do I generate ideas of things to do? Do I extend additional invitations even if others don't initiate as often as I do?"

- *Expanding conversation*: "How often do I ask thought-provoking questions that invite my friends to reflect and share more deeply? Do I in turn share my own reflections with others?"

- *Shining and letting shine*: "How practiced am I at receiving compliments and affirmation without dismissing them? How readily do I affirm my friends, validating their choices?"

- *Sharing shame*: "How frequently do I encourage my friends to share their life stresses? Am I reluctant to share my insecurities and fears?"

When I review my answers, I'm able to plot what additional acts of courage I want to embark on in the upcoming year. (These "next steps" you can add in the Vulnerability column in the Frientimacy Chart.)

Returning to the visual of the Vulnerability Compass: My ultimate goal is to have the arrows of all four vulnerabilities emanate from such a strong beating heart that they can forever push the boundaries of how far they can travel.

Vulnerability Compass

TRACKING LOVE GROWTH: My Expanding Circle

There's probably not a one of us who would argue against becoming more loving. But, more important than cheering for love is asking ourselves if we're actually growing in love. And if we are, what does that progress look like?

I do this by marking a dot in the middle of a piece of paper to represent me. I then draw a circle around that dot to illustrate how big my capacity to love others *currently* feels.

And note, this isn't about how many friends I love or whether I'm *in* love. This is a personal assessment of how *I* am showing up in this world and what kind of energy I'm putting out.

Ultimately, my goal is to expand that circle more and more every year. In order to do that I reflect at length on three words: *receptive, revealing,* and *reconciling,* asking myself questions like the following:

- *Receptive*: "Have I expanded the type of people I love? Can I honestly say I am more accepting of others than I was last year? Do I show up with less skepticism, judgment, or fear than I used to?"

- *Revealing*: "Am I able to be more vulnerable, more intimate, more real, with more people? Am I more willing not only to hear others' stories but also to share my own? And likewise, am I invoking the vulnerability of others by listening deeply, validating, and proving to be a safe person for others?"

- *Reconciling*: "Do I offer forgiveness quickly and fully? Am I someone who wages war, picks fights, and belittles others—or do I practice being someone who unites, creates harmony, uplifts, and verbally values my competitors?"

The more I am able to answer "yes" to such questions, the bigger I can draw my circle.

And while these words do serve as a measure of my growth, I also use them as a prayer for who I am becoming—who I want to become. These three words help me to invite people in, to show up with honesty, and to practice being an imperfect person with others.

Of course, these are the words that work for me; you should select words that are meaningful to you. The important thing is that you grade yourself against the person you want to be—so that you can courageously commit yourself to the actions that will ensure a wider circle in each upcoming year.

Epilogue

Friendships Can Save the World

When I picture a world in which everyone's love circle is vast and all frientimacy triangles are full, a world that each year sees greater demonstrations of courageous vulnerability—I see a world of healthy people. Healthy because they are in touch with themselves, loving to others, and surrounded by friendships that matter.

Friendships can save the world. Substantial research has demonstrated that those with strong social relationships live longer, report being happier, recover from disease faster, and have stronger immune systems than those who report feeling disconnected. In other words, relationships boost humanity. But there's more benefit to be gleaned from relationships than just additional years alive and kicking; hopefully we are also becoming more mature, loving, confident, and forgiving. This is especially important given that we can't develop entirely on our own. No therapy, meditation practice, or journaling regimen can provide the place to practice building the emotional muscles of our best selves—only the people in our lives can gift us with that space. And as we embody more of those qualities, and feel greater support and cheering from those who know us well—we can rise up and make the contribution to this planet each of us is meant to make.

I hope you will join me in this quest. Together, we can save the world.

(*To see my video sharing my manifesto "Friendships Can Save the World," please visit https://youtu.be/EHDaDy50ayU.*)

Acknowledgments

Your names don't appear in this book, but it is because of you, my girl-friends, that I wanted to write this book. It's in our time together—when we go deep and show up with utter honesty, when we laugh so hard our sides hurt, when we console each other's tears—that I think to myself: *I want everyone to have this*.

This isn't to say it's been all pom-poms and sap. Indeed, we've disappointed each other, not lived up to hopes or expectations, and gotten annoyed and triggered by each other. Because of how we've gone through it all, I think to myself: *Everyone* needs *this*.

To all of my friends: I am so grateful to be one of your friends. J'Leen, Karen, Krista, and Valerie (a.k.a. my "SoCal Girls Group"—even though most of us don't live there anymore!)—for well over a decade we've reunited once a year to spend precious time together; may every decade only get sweeter. Sher—our weekly phone calls and your deep wisdom anchor me; thank you. Daneen—it feels like we've been friends for life, which speaks highly of how you've navigated so many life changes to always value staying close—it means so much. To my 10/10 group—to meet monthly with such powerhouses inspires me to no end, and to know we've got each other's backs pushes me forward. Christine—whether weekly or monthly—our conversations have always elevated me and modeled to me how important it is to shine brightly. To my sisters, Kerry and Kati: given how different we are, if we weren't related we might not have chosen each other, but what a loss that would have been; I'm so grateful that blood bonded us and that we took it from there. Not every friendship lasts forever, but you have my word that ours will. So many names spring to mind as I think of people I love to be with: Amy, Ayesha, Bruce & Robert, Christine, Heather, Jaime, Jay & Rick, Kat, Kim, Maggie, Marney, Michelle, Miriam, Peggy & Richard, Sam, Supriya, Teggin, Tonya, and Vania—I am rich in friends.

But before I had friends, I had family. A family that filled my heart with good memories and instilled in me the knowledge that I am deeply loved even if I am a bit "much." Ha! And even the memories that aren't stellar have become sweet because of how we've grown each other, forgiven each other, and encouraged our differences in each other. It is family that frequently proves the point of this book: That if we'd be willing to stay in relationship with people, even when they disappoint us, we could experience such safety, trust, and intimacy on the other side of those hard times. Those moments are now few and far between but I promise you that, whether it's laughter or pain—I'm so grateful to call you family: Jeff & Marilyn Emery, Jenny & Jim McBride, Kerry & Mike Pate, Katrina & Jesse Emery, Dwight & Karen Nelson, Kari & Keith Jacobson, Eydie Watts, Vaughn & Becky Nelson, Natalie & Geoff Nelson-Blake, and Julian Nelson & Haidee Ortiz.

To Greg Nelson: friend, family, my husband, and so much more, you are undoubtedly the person who most helped me think through what I felt called to say in these chapters. Your thought-provoking questions, unwavering support, and tenacious ability to brainstorm with me collectively helped birth this book, your fingerprints apparent on every page. But even more indelible is your mark on my life—I am far more mature, compassionate, loving, and filled with joy because I've been loved so well by you.

And while it may be for all the above people that I *wanted* to write this book, and who inspired the learnings in this book—it is because of the lineup of talent at Seal Press that I actually *did* write this book! I am honored to be one of their authors and grateful for the encouraging and professional team who surrounded my every step. I was given complete freedom to write where I felt compelled to go, and they then turned around and helped me say it so much better. Thank you Laura Mazer, foremost, for being the midwife of this book—I adore and respect the way you work. And thank you for bringing the brilliant editing work of Kirsten Janene-Nelson to my book— that woman wowed me with her ability to not only make me more concise (not an easy job!) but to also help me communicate in a way that hopefully matters to far more people. Readers: if you like this book—you have these two women to thank. To everyone at Seal, from design to marketing: thank you. And sincere appreciation to my agent Sharlene Martin for introducing me to this dream team.

Finally, though this book was inspired by all the names above, it wasn't written for any of them. It was written for you: a woman who dares to believe that her friendships can be even more meaningful, sustaining, and fulfilling. Thank you for being one more woman in this world willing to practice showing up in ways that matter. Your actions will change your own life, those of your friends, and truly those of this world. The more women we have in this world who know their value and feel supported—the better this whole world will be. Much love to you.

Appendix

Friendship Resources

Online Friendship Matching Site: GirlFriendCircles.com

Since research reports we replace half our close friends every seven years, it's imperative throughout our lives to meet new people and develop new friendships. Whatever brings you to seek new friendships, GirlFriendCircles.com introduces you to other awesome women equally eager to meet you. (*Use the code SHASBK to save $10 off a six- or twelve-month membership at www.Girl FriendCircles.com.*)

Friendship Curriculum

"The Friendships You've Always Wanted: Learning a Better Way to Meet Up, Build Up, and Break Up with Your Friends"

Though so much of our happiness is linked to our ability to create meaningful relationships, few of us have ever taken a class on friendship. Now you can. *The Friendships You've Always Wanted* is a thirteen-week online class for women who want to build a healthy circle of friends. The course offers thirteen interviews with psychologists, authors, sociologists, and other relationship experts and a workbook to help you apply what you're learning. (*Use the code SHASBK to save 20% off this virtual class at www.FriendshipsWanted.com.*)

Book

Friendships Don't Just Happen: The Guide to Creating a Meaningful Circle of Girlfriends

While the book in your hands is about deepening your friendships, Shasta's first book focused more on how to start friendships. It includes her Five Circles of Friends, discussing the different types of friends as well as healthy expectations for various levels of friendship. Shasta expertly walks readers through the steps of both meeting friendly people and developing some chosen friendships into becoming BFFs.

Travel with New Friends: TravelCircles

GirlFriendCircles.com sponsors travel trips for women, by women, and about women to places all over the world! Whether we seek a rare and stimulating journey to Cuba, the meaning of the Middle East, or an adventurous trip to Peru or Costa Rica, we share experiences that connect us with women in each country—then return home with new friendships forged from our time together. (*To see upcoming destinations, visit www.womenstravelcircles.com.*)

Shasta's Mailing List and Friendship Blog

Past posts have included: "Top Three Tips for Making New Friends," "How to Start a Women's Circle," and "Help! Should I tell My Friend That Her Husband Is Cheating on Her?" (*Sign up to be added to the subscription list where you'll receive semiweekly inspiration and be informed of upcoming events in your area: www.ShastasFriendshipBlog.com.*)

Connect with Shasta

ADVICE: Want advice on a friendship problem? Fill out the form here: http://tinyurl.com/ShastasAdvice.

SOCIAL MEDIA: Want to engage on social media?
- https://twitter.com/ShastaMNelson
- www.facebook.com/GirlFriendCircles
- www.pinterest.com/GFCircles/
- www.youtube.com/user/ShasGFC

QUESTIONS OR COMMENTS: Want to invite Shasta to speak, have a question for her, or want to tell her what you thought of this book? Reach her here: www.girlfriendcircles.com.

References Cited

Ahlers, Amy and Arylo, Christine. *Reform Your Inner Mean Girl: 7 Steps to Stop Bullying Yourself and Start Loving Yourself*. Portland: Atria Books/Beyond Words, 2015.

Arylo, Christine. *Madly in Love with ME: The Daring Adventure of Becoming Your Own Best Friend*. Novato, CA: New World Library, 2012.

Bradberry, Travis, and Jean Greaves. *Emotional Intelligence 2.0*. San Diego, CA: TalentSmart, 2009.

Brafman, Ori, and Rom Brafman. *Click: The Forces Behind How We Fully Engage with People, Work, and Everything We Do*. New York: Crown Business, 2010.

Brown, Brené. *Daring Greatly: How the Courage to Be Vulnerable Transforms the Way We Live, Love, Parent, and Lead*. New York: Gotham Books, 2012.

Buettner, Dan. *The Blue Zones Solution: Eating and Living Like the World's Healthiest People*. Washington, D.C.: National Geographic, 2015.

Cacioppo, John T., and William Patrick. *Loneliness: Human Nature and the Need for Social Connection*. New York: Norton, 2008.

Chapman, Gary. *The Five Love Languages: How to Express Heartfelt Commitment to Your Mate*. Chicago: Northfield Publishing, 1992.

Christakis, Nicholas A., and James H. Fowler. *Connected: The Surprising Power of Our Social Networks and How They Shape Our Lives*. New York: Little, Brown and Company, 2009.

Covey, Stephen. *The 7 Habits of Highly Effective People: Powerful Lessons in Personal Change*. New York: Simon & Schuster, 1989.

Florida, Richard. *Who's Your City?: How the Creative Economy Is Making Where to Live the Most Important Decision of Your Life*. New York: Basic Books, 2009.

Fredrickson, Barbara. *Positivity: Groundbreaking Research Reveals How to Embrace the Hidden Strength of Positive Emotions, Overcome Negativity, and Thrive*. New York: Crown Archetype, 2009.

Grant, Adam. *Give and Take: A Revolutionary Approach to Success*. New York: Viking, 2013.

Hawkins, David R. *Power vs. Force: The Hidden Determinants of Human Behavior*. Carlsbad, California: Hay House, 2012.

Holland, Julie. *Moody Bitches: The Truth About the Drugs You're Taking, The Sleep You're Missing, The Sex You're Not Having, and What's Really Making You Crazy*. New York: Penguin Books, 2015.

Kushner, Harold S. *Conquering Fear: Living Boldly in an Uncertain World*. New York: Knopf, 2009.

Levine, Amir and Heller, Rachel. *Attached: The New Science of Adult Attachment and How It Can Help You Find—and Keep—Love*. New York: Tarcher, 2012.

Lieberman, Matthew D. *Social: Why Our Brains Are Wired to Connect*. New York: Broadway Books, 2013.

Martinez, Mario. *The MindBody Code: How to Change the Beliefs that Limit Your Health, Longevity, and Success*. Boulder, Colorado: Sounds True, 2014.

McGraw, Phillip C. *Relationship Rescue: A Seven-Step Strategy for Reconnecting with Your Partner*. New York: Hyperion, 2000.

Miller, Donald. *Scary Close: Dropping the Act and Finding True Intimacy*. Nashville: Thomas Nelson Publishers, 2014.

Mohr, Tara, *Playing Big: Find Your Voice, Your Mission, Your Message*. New York: Gotham Books, 2014.

Nelson, Shasta. *Friendships Don't Just Happen! The Guide to Creating a Meaningful Circle of Girlfriends*. Nashville: Turner Publishing, 2013.

Peck, M. Scott. *The Road Less Traveled: A New Psychology of Love, Traditional Values and Spiritual Growth*. New York: Touchstone Books, 1978.

Pillay, Srinivasan S. *Life Unlocked: 7 Revolutionary Lessons to Overcome Fear*. New York: Rodale Books, 2010.

Putnam, Robert D. *Bowling Alone: The Collapse and Revival of American Community*. New York: Simon & Schuster, 2000.

Rath, Tom. *Vital Friends: The People You Can't Afford to Live Without*. New York: Gallup Press, 2006.

Rath, Tom, and Jim Harter. *Wellbeing: The Five Essential Elements*. New York: Gallup Press, 2010.

Riso, Don, and Russ Hudson. *The Wisdom of the Enneagram: The Complete Guide to Psychological and Spiritual Growth for the Nine Personality Types*. New York: Bantam, 1999.

Rankin, Lissa. *Mind Over Medicine: Scientific Proof That You Can Heal Yourself*. Carlsbad, CA: Hay House, 2013.

Rubin, Gretchen. *The Happiness Project: Or, Why I Spent a Year Trying to Sing in the Morning, Clean My Closets, Fight Right, Read Aristotle, and Generally Have More Fun*. New York: HarperCollins, 2009.

Sandberg, Sheryl. *Lean In: Women, Work, and the Will to Lead*. New York: Knopf, 2013.

Schucman, Helen. *A Course in Miracles*. Temecula, California: Foundation for Inner Peace, 2012.

Turkle, Sherry. *Alone Together: Why We Expect More from Technology and Less from Each Other*. New York: Basic Books, 2011.

Vanderkam, Laura. *168 Hours: You Have More Time Than You Think*. New York: Penguin Group, 2010.

Williams, Kipling D. *Ostracism: The Power of Silence*. New York: Guilford Press, 2002.

Williamson, Marianne. *A Return to Love: Reflections on the Principles of "A Course in Miracles."* New York: HarperCollins, 1992.

About the Author

SHASTA NELSON is passionate about all things friendship. As founder and CEO of GirlFriendCircles.com—the female-friendship matching site in over sixty cities throughout North America where women of all ages go to make local friends—she speaks and writes regularly on this important topic.

She is also the author of *Friendships Don't Just Happen! The Guide to Creating a Meaningful Circle of Girl-Friends*. Her spirited and soulful voice can also be read at www.Shastas FriendshipBlog.com and in her relationship health column in *The Huffington Post*. She also gives keynote addresses, teaches workshops, and hosts Friendship Accelerator events across the United States.

She's been interviewed on the *Today* show, Katie Couric's show *Katie*, *The Early Show*, and on *Fox Extra*. She's been consulted on friendship matters by writers and reporters from such magazines as *Cosmopolitan, More, Real Simple, Redbook*, and *Good Housekeeping* and from such newspapers as *The New York Times, Chicago Tribune*, and the *San Francisco Chronicle*.

But while her work is incredibly meaningful and important to her, it is her relationships that mean the most. She's married to her best friend, Greg Nelson, is honored to be a stepmom to his three amazing kids, and is encircled by girlfriends, family members, and a community that enrich her life. They not only are the gym where she practices growing into a more compassionate, brave, and loving person—they are the people whose laughter and deep conversations fill her life and her soul.